PRACTICAL PRAYING

Practical Praying

Linette Martin

William B. Eerdmans Publishing Company
Grand Rapids, Michigan / Cambridge, U.K.

© 1997 Linette Martin
Published 1997 by Wm. B. Eerdmans Publishing Co.
255 Jefferson Ave. S.E., Grand Rapids, Michigan 49503 /
P.O. Box 163, Cambridge CB3 9PU U.K.

Printed in the United States of America

02 01 00 99 98 97   7 6 5 4 3 2 1

Library of Congress Cataloging-in-Publication Data

Martin, Linette.
    Practical praying / Linette Martin.
      p.   cm.
    Includes index.
    ISBN 0-8028-4233-X (alk. paper)
    1. Prayer — Christianity. I. Title.
BV215.M28   1997
248.3'2 — dc21   96-49760
            CIP

Biblical quotations in this book are from the New International
Version of the Bible, © 1978, New York Bible Society, and are
used by permission.

The "Eighteen Benedictions" are from *The Authorised Daily Prayer
Book,* revised edition, Bloch Publishing Company, NY, 1959, and
are used by permission.

Contents

Introduction

Praying Seemed a Waste of Time

I used to be in contact with Christians who told me that prayer was talking to God. So, following their example, I talked. Prayer was a monologue: I pleaded with God or told him in great detail what to do, pitting my will against his with the phrase "in Jesus' name" flashed into his face like a magic talisman.

As months and years went by, I became increasingly cynical about that phrase. Jesus had said, "I will do whatever you ask in My name," and there was the biblical reference to prove it: John 14:13,14. I had used the words I'd been told to use — so why didn't they work? Maybe I should have meant them more sincerely. I examined my motives, trimmed down my requests, and used the phrase again. When my prayer still didn't work, I began to put more weight on the words "if it is your will." Now I was in a catch-22. The Bible and Christian friends told me I ought to pray; so I did, but nothing happened. The alternative was to let God do what he was going to do in any case. Either way, prayer seemed a waste of time. What I found confusing was that praying was one of the things committed Christians did. There were (as I thought then) occasional answers to prayer, and the Christians I was with had similar experiences that they were happy to talk about in great detail. For me, things went from bad to worse: monologue prayers were boring, and prayer meetings were embarrassing. I would have found it easier to take all my clothes off in a roomful of people than to pray aloud in front of them.

I was told that prayer was listening as well as talking. So I listened, and discovered that it was all too easy to fantasize a conversation between myself and God. The convolutions of the human mind were so frightening that it seemed safer to stop praying. What I didn't realize was that I hadn't begun.

What little I have discovered since then I have discovered the long, hard way — here a line and there a line, with many mistakes. Once I got free from the definition "prayer is talking to God," I began to move forward. What I have learned is in this book, and I suggest practical things so prayer is built into your life gradually. All that I dare to say is, "This and thus has helped me to meet God. Try it, it may help you too."

Theologians and sociologists could argue for hours about why people pray. What is unarguable is that people do pray; whether it is for help or is an expression of thankfulness or love or rage, prayer is humanity's most basic cry. Babies show their feelings with simple sounds (for help, thankfulness, love, or rage), and tiny children babble assorted words. Then they gradually grow into clear-speaking adults who are able to construct sentences that express all their thoughts.

Just as language between human beings has to be

learned, from the babblings of an infant up to the finest verbal expression, so prayer language between a human being and the personal God has to be learned. No one in this world will learn it fully, but let us begin.

Chapter 1

The Uncontrollable God

God is not your puppet, neither are you his: that is what makes Christian prayer a strenuous and disturbing business.

When you and I were children, we had a teddy bear or an imaginary friend, and the relationship was safe because it was completely under our control. We could speak our thoughts and speak the answers back, knowing that the other would always be ready to listen. You know the kind of people who want to impose their ideas on someone else; they want a teddy-bear relationship, and when it doesn't work out, they become dictatorial or sulky. Their teddy bear didn't squeak at the right moment.

We've all met adults who have become stuck in that relationship, dictating other people's behavior to suit themselves, unable or afraid to release themselves to other people's reality. We are all capable of dropping into that mode from time to time, because the otherness of other people can be surprising and challenging, testing our opinions and patience to the limit. But that's real friendship, that's where it grows.

Christian prayer is not like cuddling a stuffed toy. God is real and uncontrollable: As C. S. Lewis says, he is not safe but he is good. We live with the eternal paradox that the God who dwells in unapproachable light is approachable.

God is approachable, but to think of the relationship that way is not satisfying to some people. They don't want someone as ordinary as Jesus Christ — fishing with his friends, his sandals muddy and the wind ruffling his hair. The Incarnation is too mundane for their refined sensibilities. Unlike God, they are above such things. Their God is safe, because he is so far away that he might as well not be there at all. They drift along with their heads high, only to stumble over a village carpenter cooking breakfast beside a lake.

God Incarnate is God on ground level, and if we can move towards him, he can move towards us. That is worrying, because we would often prefer to be left alone. It is splendid to have a God we can talk to whenever *we* wish, but it is highly inconvenient to have one who is free to walk into our lives and rearrange them whenever *he* chooses. We could bolt the door and huddle nearer to our fire, but since a personal God is everywhere, there is nowhere to hide. He made the wood which made the door: it knows his voice. The close domesticity of the Creator is precisely one of the fearful things about him. Maybe only in heaven will familiarity and awe be resolved.

When people pray, they are not talking to a teddy bear in the sky. God is who he is, and he will not be controlled. When we begin to perceive that, we will be either driven away from prayer or drawn towards it.

As gently as the growing of a plant

There are Christians who say you must go through a conversion experience (by implication, with *them* and into *their* denomination) before you can know God or pray. I disagree. Every human being can speak to the Creator and can find that he is not unknowable at all. Just as there is a God-shaped gap in everyone, so there is a God-shaped ability to communicate with the Incarnate Creator, no matter what our starting point may be. All that a conversion experience may do for some people is to jump-start them into an awareness of that, but a jump-start is not good for everyone. So think instead about simply growing towards prayer as gently and naturally as the growing of a plant.

We learn to know God in the same ways we learn to know another human being. When you stop to think about it, how else could we know the Incarnate? We look and we like what we see; we spend more time together in speech and in silence; we meet one another's friends and find interests in common. If anything has been written, we read it with attention; we share experiences, good and bad; we listen to what mutual friends say and watch how our new acquaintance speaks and acts with someone else. We grow closer to that person, unconsciously reproducing in ourselves what we see as the best in them. Slowly we become more involved in the relationship until we commit ourselves to the one we have learned to love. From then on, it is a matter of being faithful to that commitment through thick and thin, knowing that although feelings will fluctuate, a promise is made to last.

Often the commitment is no more than a gentle, interior decision to begin living towards God. The thought, "I would like to do it somehow," becomes a small, identifiable moment of choice: "Yes, I will." Conversion means a change of direction, like the movement of a ship curving around till it points towards the harbor; there is a moment when a hand is laid on the tiller and held there, and from then on the vessel moves with a new orientation.

That change of direction can happen at any age. The writer Eleanor Farjeon became a Christian at the age of seventy; she told a friend, "I feel very young and very old, and exactly the same and quite different." Later she wrote:

> Morning has broken like the first morning;
> Blackbird has spoken like the first bird.
> Praise for the singing, praise for the morning!
> Praise for them springing fresh from the
>   Word. . . .

When we meet God, he sees to it that we meet ourselves, and for many people it is hard to know which confrontation is the more unnerving — not that there is much need to worry, because daily life conspires with the Devil to protect us from either meeting. All that we have to do is to keep busy and (if we are churchgoers) keep smiling and do what is expected by the other members of the congregation.

People outside the Christian subculture think that prayer is an occupation suited to the old and the sick, a harmless pastime like eating baby food and being wrapped in a shawl. Phrases from some hymns support that view. "Sweet hour of prayer! Sweet hour of prayer that calls me from a world of care!" may sound comforting, but there is no muscle in it. In fact, there is a more bracing world out there, a great, wild, rich landscape that saints and mystics have explored. Some of them have sent messages back to base, describing the terrain, warning of dangers, and mapping some of the paths.

Prayer is not safe because God is not safe

When the Apostle Peter began to realize Jesus' power, he was afraid, saying, "Go away from me, Lord; I am a sinful man!" (Luke 5:8). Before mercy is understood (though we can never fully understand it), that is a very healthy reaction. Isaiah described the feelings of sinners in the hands of an angry God: "Go into the rocks, hide in the ground from the dread of the Lord and the splendor of his majesty!" (Isaiah 2:10).

> I saw the Lord seated on a throne, high and exalted, and the train of his robe filled the temple. Above him were seraphs, each with six wings: With two wings they covered their faces, with two they covered their feet, and with two they were flying. And they were calling to one another: "Holy, holy, holy is the Lord Almighty; the whole earth is full of his glory." At the sound of their voices the doorposts and thresholds shook and the temple was filled with smoke. "Woe to me!" I cried. (Isaiah 6:1-5)

The Apostle John described what he saw:

> . . . someone "like a son of man," dressed in a robe reaching down to his feet and with a golden sash

round his chest. His head and hair were white like wool, as white as snow, and his eyes were like blazing fire. His feet were like bronze glowing in a furnace, and his voice was like the sound of rushing waters. In his right hand he held seven stars, and out of his mouth came a sharp double-edged sword. His face was like the sun shining in all its brilliance. When I saw him, I fell at his feet as though dead. (Revelation 1:12-17)

The men who wrote those words had come face to face with the blinding glory of Christ: they spoke of what they had seen and heard. When we pray, we are approaching this God and not anyone less, so being afraid of prayer is an excellent beginning. I feel more in common with someone who says that prayer is frightening than with someone who murmurs that it is always such a sweet comfort. It is a relationship so rich that we need to bring all of ourselves to it: it will involve heart and mind, eyes and ears, speech and silence and movement, our own words and the words of others; there will be exploration and evaluation, discipline, discovery, and delight.

Six hundred years ago an English monk wrote this stringent advice to a praying friend:

Let me start by saying that the best thing you can do when you start to pray, however long or short your prayer is to be, is to tell yourself, and mean it, that you are going to die at the end of your prayer. I am not joking when I tell you this. . . . So if you want to pray wisely, or "sing psalms with all your art" [sic], as the psalmist counsels you to do, make sure that you work your mind into embracing this proper fear of the Lord. . . . (Walter Hinton, *The Letter on Prayer*)

We pray for any of three good reasons: fearful love, habit, or need. Because our lives change, one or other may be uppermost at any one time.

Fearful Love

Fear and love seem like opposite ends of a line, but in prayer that line becomes a circle. Begin where you are, travel in either direction, and you will come to the other side. Fear and love, love and fear, are like the wheels whirling within wheels that Ezekiel saw (Ezekiel 1:15-28). To love what is greater than ourselves should be a fearful experience if we have a proper sense of proportion. Some people have ridiculed medieval peasants for portraying God as a bearded old man, but are we any better imagining the Creator of the universe as a benevolent Daddy at our beck and call? The Prophets and Apostles and the makers of icons would weep and howl at such idolatry. We may become so busy being friendly with God that we forget who he is — and that would be dangerous.

Medieval craftsmen pictured God as the Ancient of Days with the abode of the eternally blessed on his right hand and everlasting hell on his left. Worship was not presented as an easy activity, and there was no attempt at making it fun. One look at the Almighty Creator and you were hammered into the ground with adoration, which is a word that means fearful love.

Habit

People who pray out of habit have understood that prayer is so important that they must do it whether they feel like it or not. Habit will tide us over when faith is at a low ebb, which means that it has the added advantage of taking our eyes off ourselves and our passing waves of scepticism.

Several people were asked what they do if it was announced that the world would come to an end in five minutes' time. The most realistic answer to the question was from an Englishwoman who said she would gather her family and pets around her and start making tea. The point was that in the midst of a crisis the mind moves to familiar patterns. When life becomes hard, there is room only for the habitual actions — like getting dressed, brushing teeth, and (if you are English) making tea. If one of those habitual actions is prayer, you will have done well.

Acquiring a habit of prayer as an adult will take a little more effort than it would for a child, but an adult mind is capable of more effort. Start where you are. To say that God is omnipresent may sound like a cold, abstract theological statement, but, like the true statements of Christian theology, it is rich and warm and alive. He is not waving at you from over yonder somewhere, or from where you wish you were, or from where you might be some day. He is waiting to meet you where you are, wherever that is. To say he is everywhere is to say he is where you are now. To say he is everywhere is to say he is with you in your present situation — whatever that situation is.

Need

To pray because of need is the most human reason of all. Before we say "Holy, holy, holy" or "Thank you," we say "Please," like a child holding out its arms for nourishment or love. Need is the motive for prayer that is closest to the human heart; it is also the one most likely to be tainted with pure selfishness, because it is very hard to distinguish between "Please" and "I want."

A long, honest look at our motives will help us see the difference. After that, the active wish for God's will is something that can be acquired only by hard labor in prayer. Even in human relationships we don't naturally want others to have their own way at our expense, and it is the same in our relationship with God. When we protest that something is unfair, it is seldom real justice that we are crying for, but something much smaller; we insist on our "rights" at every turn. To know, in theory, that God's will is the best possible for us doesn't obliterate our innate selfishness — it only makes the conscience stir fitfully like a sleepy puppy that has been prodded. "Yes, yes, of course," we say, "God's will is best." Then the next word we say is, "But . . . ," and our conscience sinks back into its comfortable snooze.

By putting your heart-needs into words, the real self-centeredness of your prayers will become all too apparent. Tell God everything that you can bring yourself to admit, then begin to line up your prayers with his will. Because he knows you perfectly, there is nothing you can say that can shock him or surprise him. Tell him exactly what you want and why. Think hard: what is your motive for asking what you just asked for? Not your self-justification but your real motive. "I want this or that because my neighbors would think well of me." "I want this because I need to accomplish something I can be proud of." "I want this because people know I am praying for it and they will be impressed by an answer." "I want this because it would make my life easier even though it would make that other person's life harder."

Praying that way is like peeling an onion, layer within layer, that makes the eyes sting. "My Father, am I really so terrible?"

"My child, I am sorry to say that you are. Now don't be afraid; you and I will work this out together."

✛   ✛

Is prayer possible in your everyday life? I believe it is, no matter what kind of everyday life you have now. Whether you have a full-time job, or a houseful of children, or are living in prison or in pain, regular daily prayer is possible. Bear with me, step by step, while we work out the details together.

Chapter 2

The Prayer of Smiles and Glances

When I was being prepared for Confirmation, I was told I ought to pray every day, and I believed it was true. The trouble was that no one told me how to do it. I thought of it as something to be done first thing in the morning or last thing at night, kneeling beside the bed with a book of words to recite. Someone who has been raised in another tradition of the church might think of it as something to be done sitting in a chair with an open Bible and chatting to God as though to a favorite uncle.

If you have been trying to pray in either of those ways and are heartily and secretly sick of it, then stop. Put aside the special sessions for now and instead try only the smallest and simplest kind of prayer that there is: the loving glance towards God. (If you are of that growing band of adults who can look back to a childhood with virtually no Christian teaching, this is where you, too, can start.)

I know this is the opposite advice from what is usually given. If people admit that they find it hard to

11

pray, the usual response is, "Aha! Maybe you are harbor-ing a secret sin! Go on retreat! Go to confession! Get born again! Ask for the gift of tongues! Read this book! Attend that conference! Listen to this tape! Listen to this preacher! Try harder!" Instead of that, the question should be, "*How* have you been trying to pray?" If the method has been wrong for you, the solution to the difficulty will not be by making more effort in the same direction.

If you limit prayer to a couple of quick sessions morning and evening, or morning only, it will take a great effort to do more. People who feel concerned about this try to make up for lost time: they map out a heavy prayer schedule complete with a subject for meditation, a Bible reading scheme of so-many verses a day, a set of spiritual exercises by a famous saint, and a long list of missionary needs. Soon they find it is all too much to do. The structure that was supposed to help them lies heavy on them.

They may attend a conference or a retreat, hoping that in some mysterious way they will return home transformed into men and women of prayer. Once the influence of two or three days fades, they find they are not transformed; the life that they return to is exactly the same as it was before they packed their weekend suitcase, and the influences against prayer are as strong as ever. They may look wistfully towards the charismatic movement, wondering if there is some secret there that they have missed. They read biographies of great men and women of God, but, instead of feeling inspired to go and do likewise, they feel belittled and hopeless. I remember thinking that if one more person told me how John Wesley got up every day at 4:00 a.m. to pray, I would scream till all the church windows broke and would never sing any of his brother's hymns again.

When high standards of prayer seem out of reach, sorrow takes over. Prayer is something that you tried but found you could not get into. You begin to think it may be some strange, rare knack like a gardener's green thumb. You can be put off prayer in one of two ways: either you are told repeatedly how vital it is, till you are afraid of failing, or you are told how easy it is and, when you find it is not, you are too afraid or too ashamed to admit it.

Pare back to the minimum

There is no inability in you: it is just that you tried too much too soon. The fact that you tried shows that you care, and God remembers and honors every sincere attempt to reach him, no matter what the result. If any of us were to be judged by results rather than by motives, it would be unbearable. What you need now is to begin again very slowly and to go on in the same way. Pare back to the absolute minimum and, when that little is established as part of your daily life, begin to build up slowly, finding what is best for you. Prayer is too important to try to learn in a hurry.

To approach God by the prayer of smiles and glances is such a gentle method that love will grow without strain. At first it may feel unsatisfying because it seems that nothing is happening, and this is the best first lesson: that prayer is not for producing nice feelings. If feelings were all that we wanted from it, cannabis or Romantic music would work faster.

As I was writing this chapter, a house at the end of our road was being restored. Planning permission had taken a long time while the old walls stood looking unwanted and unloved. Then much of it was taken down, and it seemed that it was being unbuilt rather than built. For weeks there was no visible change while piles of bricks stood in the trodden garden. But there was slow progress until even the untrained eye could see the outlines of the renewed rooms. Then the walls went higher and the roof went on. Again there was a period of no visible progress, though plenty was going on inside as plumbers and plasterers and electricians came and went. Finally, the family moved in and the real life of the house began. Building prayer into your life will be like that: at first there will be steps backwards, then there will be times of no apparent progress. It is only if you keep going slowly and steadily that something wonderful will begin to happen.

Though some Christians say they have no time to pray, I do not believe it. Everyone has time for what they believe to be important. No matter how busy we were, if someone were to convince us that it was important to juggle, or to clog dance, or to play the crumhorn every day, we would do it. Even though we might not do it well, if we were convinced it mattered, we would persevere and make time to do it by putting other activities aside.

To pray by smiles and glances will mean there is no change in your external life. Your hours of work and daily routine (or lack of it) will be untouched. You may feel a great wave of relief at finding that you can meet God in this simple way — for the wonderful fact is that you *will* meet him.

Much love can go into a single glance

To look at God is not to visualize a bearded old man sitting on a cloud. Neither Jews nor Eastern Orthodox Christians tried to make a picture of God himself. It was forbidden. God Incarnate, Jesus Christ, could be pictured in his humanity, and the Holy Spirit could be shown in symbol by a dove or by tongues of fire. The impossibility of picturing God was forgotten during the Renaissance, when God the Father was shown as a huge, bearded, half-naked figure, more Jupiter or Jove than the Trinity.

To look at God means simply, to look: I cannot explain it any other way. Give your attention to him and let your soul smile. I know that may sound fanciful and what some people would derisively call "a bit mystical," but it is something that must be done if prayer is ever to be more than either recitation or chatter. So do not analyze what it means to look at God: just do it. You can. The facility has been built into you by the God who created you.

The glancing prayer may be only, "How wonderful you are," or it may be only, "My Lord." Much love can go into a single glance. You may already be familiar with short aspirations and have found them cold and blood-less. You may have tried making a short act of faith, tossing out the occasional "Lord, have mercy" on the spur of the moment, but it has not lit any fire in you. What makes glancing prayers different is that you first look at God, then you speak. Prayer is communication. By using that word I am including the old phrase "talking to God" and have opened it out to include much more. Do you not usually look at another human being before you speak? Of course you do, and it is just the same when you speak to God.

There are lives in which this is the only kind of prayer that is possible. Those in pain or under sedation can speak to a hospital visitor only in short sentences, because neither their voice nor their mind can cope with a long thought; when they speak to God it will be in the same way. Jesus' words from the cross were as short as the raw breath of a man in agony. People read that he quoted the first words of Psalm 22 and they wonder why he did not recite more of it. It was because he was in great pain, and the first words of the Psalm stood for the whole expression of his heart.

Someone who has loved God for only a short time may still feel awkward in his presence, as timid as the young wife in an arranged marriage; so little is known of this person, what is he really like? We all fear the unknown, and who can be more unknown than a God we have never seen? Very short prayers make no demands and they are not intended to; they are the smiles of a relationship that is beginning to grow.

Many people pray this way for years while thinking that it does not really count. It does count: even short prayer is real. It is enough to love God very simply, beginning where you are. Look at him, love him, and put the present state of your heart into the fewest possible words: "We love you because you first loved us." Prayer can be much more than this, but it need never be less.

You think that everyone looks at God before they pray? Stop and think for a moment: do you? It is all too easy to spill words into the atmosphere and experience some relief from tension. Some people find that switching from set forms to a conversational style jolts them into a fresh awareness, but even a conversational style can degenerate into mere therapeutic babbling unless you look in the right direction and keep your attention fixed.

There is no need to address God with a full title every time you speak, as though he were a character in a Russian novel. Instead of saying his name, take a moment to look before you speak. Keep the glances short. Look first, "Thank you for your love." Look, then speak, "Help me to pray better." His names and titles are splendid, and you will find yourself using them in time. Do not think, though, that you must speak his name in order to get his attention: he is already nearer to you than the air you are breathing. In any case, the names you address him by will vary from day to day, depending on how you are to him and on how he is to you. Often a loving look will be enough.

There is an innate conservatism in the human mind; left to itself, it resolves life into patterns and finds security in them. Even the incurable muddler has a pattern in life, that of always losing things, always forgetting phone and fax numbers, and always being late for appointments. The mind resists any attempt to introduce a new habit, though it may enjoy a temporary novelty. Anyone who has tried a new diet or a new method of giving up smoking knows this already; for a while the novelty gives enough interest and impetus to keep them going, but before long some level of the mind rebels. A new habit has been tacked onto the familiar life, like a new patch sewn onto old cloth, and it quickly tears off. Once the novelty has faded, the familiar way of life reasserts itself with surprising force. When some extra job needs doing, the first thing that will be pushed aside to make room for it is the thing that was most recently added.

We are responsible for doing as much as we can within the shape of our lives. It is wonderful to know that private prayer is private, that there is no one standing behind you to criticize your progress. You come only to God, who knows you perfectly and loves you forever. As for you, why criticize your own progress? You are who you are, a unique combination of personality and experiences, and since there is no one like you anywhere in the world, there is no measuring rod to stand beside and feel belittled. So what if John Wesley rose at 4:00 a.m. and prayed for several hours? He went to bed much earlier than we do, in those days before electric light. Moreover, he had a special room in his house to pray in undisturbed, and he did not have to get the family's breakfast.

If glancing prayers are your only way for the next part of your pilgrimage, you will be moving forward. The pace may seem ludicrously slow compared with that of saints or famous missionaries, but if you play the comparisons game, you will lose. You can meet God where you are now, wherever that may be. Now — before you read any more — look at him and say something to him in as few as half a dozen words.

Begin to build up your relationship with God by smiles and glances, and once you are at peace with him (which precedes and leads to being at peace with yourself) there will be time to think about building in something else. For now, form the habit of praying with few words and of always looking before you speak.

✛ ✛

Look at and be looked at by the great God, Who in Trinity is worshipped and glorified, and Whom we declare to be now set forth as clearly before you as the chains of our flesh allow, in Jesus Christ our Lord, to Whom be glory for ever. Amen.

St. Gregory of Nazianzus,
4th century

Chapter 3

Time and Place

Much as we all like central heating, there is something attractive about an open fire. Though the temperature in the room may be the same in either case, an open fire is a focal point. Once you have learned to love God by praying by smiles and glances throughout the day, the wish to have a focussed time for prayer will grow in you.

As soon as you begin to think about it with a definite plan, the large busyness of the day envelops you as, from first ring of the alarm to last light out, every minute looks filled. Pray at the same time every day? It sounds like a joke. But if prayer is going to become part of your life, beyond smiles and glances, it has to happen at the same time every day. If the time is allowed to vary, it will soon wander out of your life altogether. Other tasks shout so loudly and look so important that the silent, solitary, humble task will be pushed aside.

The way to begin is slowly: I advise five minutes. That may feel impossibly short, but it is better to get a short time established than to begin with a longer one that you give up later as being impractical. It should not be longer on one day because it feels nice and shorter on another day as the mood takes you. Even if you feel great enthusiasm and want to go on longer one day, please restrict yourself to only five minutes. Set aside the same small block of time day after day after day. It can be done.

If you work outside your home, there are likely to be three periods in the day in which prayer is possible: before you go to work in the morning, during your lunch hour, or in the evening. Only you can decide which is the most practical. "How about when I'm driving?" I hear you ask. No. Drive-time is for glancing prayers, not for your daily five-minute slot. You may be able to pray when you are sitting in a public park: it depends on your ability to concentrate among children and dogs. You might consider going into a church; some, especially the Catholic and High Episcopal ones, are open during the week so anyone can go in to be quiet before God.

Praying when you have small children

The person who finds it hardest to make a regular daily time for prayer — even only five minutes — is the at-home mother or at-home father of preschool children. At-home mothers or fathers work a full day, seven days a week, in conditions of mess, stress, and hours that no labor union would accept. It's not a joke: it's very tough. One mother said, "It isn't just that you don't have time to finish a single job: you don't have time to finish a single thought!" A mother is someone who can simultaneously prepare a dog's breakfast, three packed lunches, a shepherd's costume, and a school note. Spiritually, those years can be a long dry time.

Is it possible to trade babysitting with a nearby mother so you each have five minutes with God? I don't mean praying aloud with a Christian neighbor while your combined children demolish the next room. You wonderful at-home-working mothers (*all* mothers are *working* mothers) need time alone. Can you arrange with another mother for five minutes on two fixed days of the week for several months on end? She does it for you, and you do it for her. If just the thought of it brings tears to your eyes, you really need it. See what you can arrange, even if for the first few times you feel you have wasted the minutes because your mind is full.

An occasional half-hour when a friend comes in to babysit "so you can go and pray" could easily end up being used for emergency shopping, and by being occasional would introduce yet another unpredictable element into your unpredictable days. It is important to have a time you can count on in advance. Establish a pattern. If there are only those two predictable points of five minutes in your week with small children, your whole life will regain a sense of proportion. It may be difficult to arrange, but it is possible: why not phone a friend now and both of you see what you can do?

If you are really isolated from Christian friends, go back to the chapter about glancing prayers and make it your own as thoroughly as you can. Remember that glancing prayers are not a *substitute* for the real thing: they *are* the real thing. Concentrate on developing the prayer of smiles and glances now, and when the shape of your life changes, you can go on to a more focussed time.

Testing the Rule

After a couple of weeks, again after about a month, and again still later you will find a strong resistance to the pattern that you have introduced. Don't be surprised. It is called Testing the Rule, and adults do it as much as children. It is precisely when you are tempted to give up the new habit that you must stick to it if you want it to remain a permanent pattern in your life. Stick to it re-gardless and the resistance will go away.

Recognize the hump of discouragement for what it is: the Devil's gift of worry operating through the normal human process of testing a new pattern in your life. Prayer seems a waste of time and you find that extra work emerges as though from nowhere, making a habit of prayer look supremely unimportant. You may get drawn into a legalistic system of "rob Peter to pay Paul": having missed your five minutes one day, you'll find yourself thinking, "Well, never mind; I'll pray for ten minutes tomorrow and make up for it that way." Then the Devil makes you look at arithmetic and soon you are reasoning, "Well, my weekdays are extra busy just now, so why don't I pray for about fifteen minutes on Saturday and another twenty on Sunday to make up the total of five minutes a day all through the week. Yes, good idea. I've still kept to Linette's scheme of five minutes a day, but I've lumped it all together." Please don't. Go for five minutes a day every day, at a time and place of your convenience.

If you get over the first hump of discouragement, things will go smoothly until you get to the second hump and then the third hump — and perhaps a fourth and a fifth — a little while later. But once you are over them, the new habit will have become a part of your life. Without your realizing how, priorities will have begun to rearrange themselves to make way for the new habit, instead of the other way around. Exceptional circumstances to your rule will be very rare and very short-lived, and as soon as the exception is over, your life will resolve itself back with a sense of relief to include the once-new habit. You would now be introducing a disturbing new element if you tried to give it up.

When you have set yourself a time and kept to it, you will begin to discover a sense of order. As the day goes by, you bring your current job to a stopping place so you can keep your appointment with God. You will find that the pattern of the day has brought with it an element of expectancy.

If there is no set time, your work will expand to fill the whole day, and at the end of it an air of guilt will hover about you: prayer is something that should have been done earlier and properly; you should have thought ahead; you should have made time for it, it is wrong to give God the leftovers. You throw yourself on your knees tense and tired, or you drop into a chair and seize a Bible, thinking fiercely, "Now I've really got to pray!" That is no way to come into the presence of God.

Instead, you can first plan a time to pray and then move steadily towards it day by day, though you may need several months of quiet experiment before you find the best time. You will find that prayer is no longer a thing subject to whims and emotions: your watch tells you that it is time to begin. Weekends will probably call for a different pattern than weekdays, but, here again, only you can decide.

I am still talking about five minutes, which time

will seem so short that it feels barely worthwhile. Train yourself to stick with five minutes a day for several months, and then extend the time to only ten minutes for several more months. There is no hurry. In the Western world today, and in countries influenced by the West, we live in an atmosphere of such speed and pressure that it is always safe to tell ourselves to go more slowly than we feel we should. Extend your daily time to fifteen minutes or longer only when you are sure you can use the time fully. There will be less tendency to daydream when you are aware that every minute counts.

Aesop told a story about a hare and a tortoise: you remember which one finally won the race. If it sounds as though I am trying to hold you back, that is because I want you to continue to move forward. Progress may not be obvious, and for that reason it will not be satisfying, but it will be steady progress, which is what counts. The Devil thrives on spiritual excess: he knows that if you become overexcited you will soon become tired of the idea and give it all up. Plod along like Aesop's tortoise and you will win in the end.

First thing in the morning?

Many people advise a time for prayer first thing in the morning; they enthuse about spending time on their knees in the fresh pearly hour of the day. They remind me of a James Thurber cartoon in which the wife flings open the bedroom curtains and calls gleefully to the hump in the bed, "Don't you want to greet the rosy-fingered dawn?"

Some Christians not only *advise* that you pray first

thing in the morning: they teach that it *must* be the time. I say, commit your day to God as soon as you wake, then find a five-minute slot somewhere in some daily pattern that suits your present life. This is an individual matter; if it works for you, it works.

I was in a friend's kitchen helping her to put a meal together. I looked at her shelf of carefully labelled, reused containers. "Where do you keep the rice?"

"Well, obviously, in the container labelled 'Chocolate Sprinkles.' Where do you keep yours?" The system was odd, but it was her kitchen and it worked for her.

Christians are ordinary members of the human race; some of them spring cheerfully into action at the first chirp of the alarm clock, while others know that their humanity doesn't begin to emerge until after their second cup of coffee. Though temperament can be trained and modified, it will not be obliterated. Do not let yourself be bullied by other Christians who tell you that you ought to pray at such and such a time. There is no ought about it. Accept the way that you are and work out the best time of prayer for yourself. "Give God the best of the day!" cries the up-with-the-lark Christian, but what if the first time of the morning is your worst time? You are who you are. God made many other birds besides the larks.

What do you do for five minutes?

Once you have found the time, the question arises how to fill it. The prayer of smiles and glances will have become like background music throughout your day, and now that you have a solid five minutes of prayer, what do you do? You only need to think, in a thankful way, about the love of God. Don't push yourself to have Great Religious Thoughts — just let your mind hover around the idea like a bee at a flower, or let it be like a compass needle swinging to and fro, but always returning to North.

If even that feels too strenuous, leave it for now. Stay quietly in one place and leaf through a hymnbook, and if a particular line or verse catches your eye, stay with it. You may remember one hymn that you always liked; look it up in the index of first lines and read it through at your own speed. There is no hurry; all you have to establish in your life at this stage is a short time of day given to Godward thoughts.

I recommend a hymnbook rather than a Bible at this stage, because it is too soon to attempt a scheme of ordered reading. You are still pared back to the minimum. A hymn usually develops one theme, and this can help you learn how to hold your mind steadily on one idea. What you are doing is forming a habit of focussed thought which is designed to last for the rest of your life. You may want to return to the same hymn for many days. God has a lot to teach us, and we miss most of it by being in a hurry. At the end of the five minutes, thank him for it, and then get on with the rest of your day.

After a week of this you may begin to feel like a perfect fool. You sit mulling over a hymbook for five minutes a day: where is it supposed to get you? Think again. You can allow yourself to look forward to that part of the day, and it will become as refreshing as an oasis on a long, dry journey. It will be refreshing in anticipation, in actuality, and in memory. Don't try to combine this time with the time when you relax and have a cup of tea or coffee. Prayer brings its own refreshment, but it is work; so, from the very beginning (apart from the smiles and glances), a time of daily prayer must be kept strictly separate from all the other events of the day. If you are not firm with yourself about this, the daily five minutes with God will disappear into the dregs of the coffee cup and will never be seen again.

Place

Having found a time to pray, the question of place will have arisen naturally. A place to pray offers a spatial focus just as a time to pray provides a temporal one. It will bring associations of prayer that can help you to control your leaping thoughts. Keep your hymnbook there and anything else you may add later; they will be waiting for you every day like friends ready to help. Going to that place will be a tiny homecoming where there is wonderful work to be done and much to be learned.

In his Temple dedication prayer, King Solomon referred both to God's omnipresence (everywhere-ness) and to his specific presence:

> "The heaven, even the highest heaven, can't contain you. How much less this temple I have built! Yet give attention to your servant's prayer, . . . May your eyes be open towards this temple night and day, this place of which you said, 'My Name shall be there. . . .'" (1 Kings 8:27-29)

For all their great vision of an everywhere-God, the Israelites were given a specific place in which to be aware of his presence. To say they were primitives who believed they had God in a box is to misunderstand God's self-revelation, the Jews' faith, and the human mind. The idea of a personal God being everywhere is so difficult for us to comprehend that we need locality as well as omnipresence. Without contradiction, God is everywhere and makes his presence known in a particular place. Christians who emphasize one at the expense of the other lose something wonderful.

Choosing a special place to pray makes no difference to God, because he sees and hears you wherever you are. You have already experienced this by your practice of glancing prayers, and those prayers will continue throughout the day. Place makes no difference to him. Place is for us because we are spatial people whose entire experience (apart from anaesthesia, dreams, or drugs) is with a sense of space. As physical people, we are naturally comfortable relating to what has a local habitation and a name. A fixed place to pray is no more a limitation on God than is a fixed time. It is a device that helps us to focus our mind by focussing our body, because body and mind work together.

If you are used to kneeling for prayer, you will need a piece of furniture of suitable height, or if you sit, an upright chair. The place where you choose to pray should be free from draughts, have decent light for reading, and be as quiet as possible; these things are a basic minimum. It should be free of visual distractions such as a busy street just outside the window. Whether or not you have a cross or a picture or neither is a matter of personal taste. (I'll be saying more about pictures in Chapter 9.) Like the time for prayer, the place will not be perfect, because this is not a perfect world, but see that it is the best that you can arrange.

It may seem that I am spending too much time on the stage management of prayer: lights, props, and sets. But setting is important for physical people who live and pray in a physical world. Because prayer is important and because it is so easy to be distracted from it, we need to use every possible aspect of this world to help us.

Approach your chosen place in peace. It is better to spend two minutes walking to it than two minutes trying to calm down after you have run to it. Go quietly to the place and come quietly from it; come and go as though the angels were wild birds that your movements could frighten away.

Take your shoes off. No, it is not because you are like Moses on holy ground (though the symbolism may please you). It is because when people take their shoes off they relax.

✣   ✣

We stand in the cell of self-knowledge. We know that we do not exist of ourselves but by the goodness of God in us. We acknowledge that we receive our being and the grace that is higher than our being from him.

St. Catherine of Siena,
14th century

Chapter 4

Choreography

The word "choreography" has come from ancient Greek theater, where the *choreia* (the chorus) spoke to the audience by carefully rehearsed movements. Because the open-air theater was so large, the choreography of the play was as vital a part of communication as the words. What could not be heard could at least be seen, and when something was both heard and seen, it was doubly effective.

What was true in the distant sunlit glory of Greek theater is still true: choreography speaks. When you have found the best time and place to pray every day, the next thing to discover is how choreography can help you to express yourself to God. In its broad sense, choreography is body language, which is a normal part of human relationships. We use body language every day, even on the telephone. From before the time that we learned to speak in words, we communicated in a language of movements and positions. Choreography in prayer is not an exotic extra to be indulged in only by charismatics, dancers, or other enthusiasts, but is an essential part of everyone's life. When we use it to help us pray, we are behaving towards God as the physical people that we have been created to be.

Let your body lead your mind

The position of the body can help both to focus and to express what is in your mind; it can also show a change of emphasis, as from penitence to praise. The Holy Communion Service in the 1662 Anglican *Prayerbook* requires the congregation to kneel for the Collect (which is appropriate for a prayer in the Western tradition of the church), to sit for the Epistle (because it is some teaching on the Christian life), and to stand for the Gospel (a position that shows willingness to go at once and obey a command of Jesus). The progression of kneel-sit-stand is not just an incidental shuffling so the worshippers stay awake at an early service. Instead, it expresses their relationship to the different parts of the liturgy. Words and position go together, and there is a logic in that dance. Biblical examples of prayer positions are varied: standing with the hands spread out, sitting, lying face down, or kneeling. Even if you are limited by age or physical handicap, you can visualize yourself taking up a position and can move as near to it as possible.

If your only possible time for prayer is after a heavy evening meal, you should avoid sitting bent over or kneeling upright since those positions put a strain on the middle part of your body, where your stomach is. If you are sleepy, it is best to stand or walk, and if you are a little sleepy but like to pray sitting in a chair, an upright one would be better than a big soft one. If the body is at peace the mind can concentrate because the body and the mind work together; if the body is allowed to slump, the mind will do the same

Some people who have accepted that there is a close link between thought and body in worship will try to get their thoughts in order first. They say that when they *feel* sufficiently humble or prayerful, *then* they will kneel, or when they have enough *faith, then* they will go to church. Somewhere in their minds there is an unreasonable fear of hypocrisy: they want their thoughts to lead the body.

"That's right," says the Father of Lies, "Don't be a hypocrite. God hates hypocrites. Don't pray or go to church until you believe everything."

What people have not allowed themselves to experience is that the influence can flow in the other direction, with the body leading the thoughts. The associations between body language and mental attitude are so strong that if one is changed, the other will eventually change too.

One way to learn humility before God is to put yourself in a humble position. At first it may feel like an act of hypocrisy, but if the position is thoughtfully taken and held, it will gradually influence the mind. Because mind and body are united, the influence is inevitable; recognize this fact and use your body to help you to pray.

Experiment with small movements

In some churches Christians show their praise by lifting their arms in the air. If the action is not rooted in the culture and the time, it can be very distracting to others. It may be a sincere expression of praise, or it may be exhibitionism. ("Look, everyone, I'm more full of praise than you are!") We are such complicated people that not even the person performing the action in public can always know the real reason.

Five hundred years ago, in *The Imitation of Christ,* Thomas à Kempis wrote sound advice for clergy and laity:

> When you are celebrating, do not be too slow or too quick, but observe some good practice in common with those with whom you live. You should not cause others irritation or annoyance, but observe some way in common as appointed by men of more authority, rather than your own feelings and your own devotion.

While individualism is out of place in the united dance of the liturgy, you can have all the freedom you need in private prayer. If the idea of choreography in prayer is new to you, it is wise to experiment with the smallest, gentlest movements rather than flinging yourself into something excessive like a ham actor doing Victorian melodrama. Excess that felt wildly exciting at first could fade into embarrassment and even disgust; if any movement makes you feel the least bit awkward, even in private, leave it alone at once. Awkwardness is probably an indication that you have not quite come to terms with the fact that you are a physical person at prayer; don't try too much too soon. Acknowledge that movements and positions can be used to help, without forcing yourself into anything that feels unnatural. You may change later; then again, you may never change. You are who you are: let God work with you, beginning where you are now.

Try opening your clasped hands very slowly to finish with palms upward. Half a minute by the clock may seem an impossible amount of time to spend on a simple movement, but it will be thirty seconds well spent. Though it is only a small gesture, it might be all the choreography you will ever need to use.

If making the sign of the cross does not offend you, perform the ancient movement of self-blessing with the quietness of an unrolling cumulus cloud rather than the perfunctory flicker of lightning. I have seen Orthodox Christians do this with enormously impressive dignity, combining it with two deep bows. If you are paralyzed and can move only your head, make the sign of the cross with your head, slowly from as far up as you can, to as far down as you can, then from all the way one side to the other side; then lift your face to God like an expectant child.

A sacred space

Jews, standing to recite daily prayers, mark out a sacred space by taking three steps forward then three back, and do it again at the end of the prayer to close the space. Small movements like that are a means of defining a prayer-place and a prayer-time, using place and time as means of disciplining our thoughts. The beautifully decorated doorways of Romanesque and Gothic churches are a means of defining place for us. They mark out the difference between our life of home, work, and leisure, and a specially dedicated place of worship. To step through such a door is to enter sacred space.

If you are faced with a difficult problem, you can

pray using the position and movement universally as-
sociated with grief. People in mental distress rock to and
fro as though they were a baby being rocked in their
mother's arms. Very likely it shows a wish to return to
the comforting days of pre-birth and infancy. All over
the world, sorrow and intensity are expressed by rocking
and by sitting hunched up with the knees near the face,
or by covering the face with hands or clothing. Rocking
has become the traditional movement when reading the
Torah (the movement was first noted in the Middle Ages
when it was unusually difficult to be a Jew). If a rocking
movement helps you to pray, do it gently and be ready
to ease off into stillness as God quiets you.

Some Christians find that they pray best while
walking, which is another rhythmic movement that may
be used to quiet the mind and help concentration.
Whether you regularly pray when you are walking depends on where you are able to walk. The countryside
may be helpful, or it may make your thoughts drift into
a love of the landscape. The town may be helpful, or the
shop windows and advertisements may be distracting.
Find out what works best for you. If you have been
sitting or kneeling and begin to fall asleep, keep to the
job in hand by walking about the room with measured
tread like a resigned tiger. One pastor used to escape the
distractions of his family by climbing into the attic to
pray; they would hear him pacing up and down, the
sound of his footsteps sometimes accompanied by the
pattering paws of the family cat.

I mentioned furniture in the previous chapter. If
you prefer kneeling for prayer, you must find the best
piece of furniture to kneel at. Traditionally, people have
knelt beside the bed, which offers a soft surface on which

to rest the forearms and plenty of room to put an open Bible, hymnbook, or prayerbook. The trouble is that the custom of kneeling beside beds began when beds were higher than they are now and the body could lean forward only a little with the back held in a straight line from hip to neck. If you have tried to pray beside a low modern bed, you know how your back aches after a couple of minutes.

If the bed is too low, see if a couple of firm pillows on it will bring it up to a comfortable height. Alternatively, try kneeling at a sturdy table with something on it to cushion your arms. Or with a wide windowsill, you could follow the example of the Prophet Daniel and pray at an open window (though not, of course, with any intention of showing off).

Standing for prayer, in stillness with the arms held out, may express your supplication better than any other position. In one sense, Christians do stand in the presence of God, joyously and freely accepted in the Beloved. If most of your daily work is sedentary, standing for prayer could be the best position to help keep your mind alert.

Whatever position or movement you use, go deeply into it, letting it speak for you instead of words: simple, gentle positions and movements are best, because they will bring you quietness. Since they have to be performed with a certain amount of muscle control (remember those slowly opening hands?), there is less chance that they become emotional self-indulgence to impress the angels or to feed your image of yourself as being pious. It was the priests of Baal who leaped about wildly, trying to impress their god (or maybe themselves) with their sincerity: the Prophet Elijah behaved in a different way.

If you are not very careful with a movement or position, you will find that you are looking at yourself as though in a mirror. Instead of that — whatever you do — look at God steadily the whole time. It takes practice. There is a conscious process in it that I find hard to describe: you have to become very aware of yourself in order to forget yourself. Set a watchdog to guard your self-centeredness while you attend to God.

No one else can dictate to you what position or movement you use in private prayer. So allow yourself plenty of time, relate yourself to God, and see what you discover. The positions and movements I have described either have been recorded in the Bible or have been hallowed by centuries of Christian worship. I strongly advise that you stick to those rather than trying anything exotic. Remember that the position we take makes no difference to God. He sees us the way we really are, and often we must admit, "More's the pity." Though a pious position will not deceive or impress him for a moment, it will be of immense help to you in training body and mind to speak the same language. Like the simple disciplines of time and place, positions are for your own benefit, not his.

✢   ✢

Bring to God whatever is on your mind at this moment: what position expresses it best? Maybe you visualize a figure darting a loving glance upward, or sitting in a chair and bent forward as though listening. You may see in your mind's eye someone kneeling in the traditional attitude of Christian prayer, or lifting both hands up as though holding a heavy weight or receiving a gift, or standing with arms raised in delight.

> By all means use sometimes to be alone . . .
> salute thyself: see what thy soul doth wear.

George Herbert,
The Temple, 17th century

Chapter 5

Praying Informally

"Worship the Lord in the splendor of his holiness. Tremble before him, all the earth!" (1 Chronicles 16:29, 30). What style of language expresses that worship best?

To hear Christians from a nonliturgical tradition pray their hearts out in everyday words can be a dazzling experience if you have been raised on recited formulas. Informal prayers have their feet firmly on the ground and their eyes open to the world; that is their strength. Their weakness is that they can easily become mere chatter-prayers, relying on more and more emotion to keep their freshness, and with the word "Lord" slotted in where the commas would be in a written version.

As we grow to know God better, we should expect to move towards more respectful language. Though it may be increasingly warm and simple, it should acknowledge more and more what the relationship is. A small child in a crowd is not to be blamed if he greets a monarch with "Hello," but if he grows up in the court, he will learn the fuller dimensions of the relationship. Knowing the right way to behave will give him more freedom rather than less, and the right kind of confidence will grow.

God is our Father

"Just talk to God," we are told. "Prayer is just talking
to him as to your own Daddy." I doubt if even children
are helped towards Christian worship by that naive
approach — and anyone who has been abused by their
father would be thrown into deep confusion by hearing
God likened to such a human parent. The teaching that
God is Father and Abba-father should be presented
today with compassionate awareness that, for some
people, the word "father" triggers memories of a brute.
For others, the word "mother" triggers memories of
someone uncaring, tense, and preoccupied, or of someone who did not prevent the father's abuse. Calling God
"Mother" not only would fail to help someone whose
experience of parenthood has been warped, but it is
foreign to Judeo-Christian teaching.

Because we accept God's revelation, we use male
words to describe him; he is not "it," he is not "he/she,"
he is not our heavenly Mother. He is, as the Prophet
Isaiah taught us, "Wonderful, Counsellor, Mighty God,
Everlasting Father, the Prince of Peace" (Isaiah 9:6). He
is, as Jesus Christ taught us, "Our Father in heaven"
(Matthew 6:9). We dare not dodge the rigorous reality
of revelation.

A Christian woman whose father abandoned the
family when she was seven found the fatherliness of God
when she was an adult, by reading Psalm 145. Though
the word "Father" does not appear in it, this psalm
presents the actions, care, and qualities of parenting, the
love, strength, and protective care of true maleness. "The
Lord is faithful to all his promises and loving toward all
he has made" (Psalm 145:13)

Someone who has a good human father can look at God and say, "Thank you for giving me a male parent who taught me about you." Someone who has a terrible father can look at God and say, "Thank you for being the sort of father I wish I had." God is the best that fatherliness can be, and far above all human parenting.

God is our king

Heaven is not constructed according to any human political agenda: heaven is the way it is, and though we are all saved by grace, we are not all the same. God is Lord of all. There are cherubim and seraphim, who are different and unequal from one another in creation, status, and function; there are archangels and there are angels in several orders. There is Christ, made in his incarnation to be a little lower than the angels; there is his mother, to whom an archangel said, "Blessed are you among women." There are prophets and apostles from the Old and New Testaments, there are men and women saints from every generation and walk of life — and there is us. The early Christian makers of icons and the painters of medieval murals represented heaven as a place of eternal hierarchies. The King of Angels is our everlasting king and we are his subjects, known individually, loved and safe.

Appropriate ways of addressing the Lord of Glory will develop communication rather than cramp it, so do not despise the graciousness of good language; there must be discipline if there is to be delight. If we teach people to relate to Christ as to their next-door neighbor, we risk obscuring them from the Reality that they have knelt down to reach.

The concept of majesty has been lost

Is it proper to address God as "you" rather than "thou"? The real issue lies deeper than pronouns. A Shakespeare sonnet could be rewritten in the "you" form without substantially changing its rhythm or meaning. ("Shall I compare you to a summer's day? You are more lovely and more temperate. . . .") The Daily Service that has been broadcast without a break by the British Broadcasting Corporation since 1928 changed the wording of its prayers from "thou" to "you" about fifty years later, but because the reverent tone of the prayers continued the same, many regular listeners either failed to notice the difference or did not complain.

It does not matter if we say, "We have offended against thy holy laws," or "We have offended against your holy laws." What matters is that we recognize the galactic enormity of our offense. If modern prayers and modern liturgies fail to raise us to God, it is not because of a change of pronouns. It is because we have lost the concept of majesty. We understand enthusiasm and we are familiar with friendliness and equality. But when it comes to praying with deep reverence, we need to re-learn the language of priests and kings.

> Almighty God, our heavenly Father,
> maker of all things, judge of all people;
> we confess to you with sorrow our many sins
>   and wicked acts,
> which we have done deliberately
> by thought, word and deed
> against your divine majesty.
> We have stirred up your wrath

and indignation against us:
now we earnestly repent, and are sorry
with a full heart
for all that we have done wrong.
The memory of our sins is a grief to us;
the burden is too heavy to be borne.
Have mercy on us, have mercy on us,
    most merciful Father;
for your Son our Lord Jesus Christ's sake,
    forgive us all that is past,
and give us the grace, from this time on,
to serve and please you in lives renewed;
to the honour and glory of your Name,
through Jesus Christ our Lord.

(General Confession,
1662 Anglican Communion,
author's modernization)

If you find yourself reacting against older forms of prayer, stop and consider whether "all the thees and thous" are really the reason. Could it be that the content of the older forms makes them more searching to say? We will not learn adoration by fellowship but by fear. Language is a clothing for our thoughts; it is something we can use, rather than allowing it to use us the wrong way. As with clothes, both formality and informality have their appropriate places.

Honesty and simplicity

Instead of reading modern books of informal prayers, I suggest you read Bible prayers (there is a list on pages

160-74 of this book) and those found in classic church Prayerbooks. Read them and reread them, and absorb their style. There is often a twofold pattern of petition and praise, with the needs of the moment compacted into a few words. Men and women in the Bible expressed themselves to God with disarming honesty and simplicity, never with crude informality, and the classic prayers of the church have the same honest dignity. They show a deep understanding that the fear of the Lord is the beginning of wisdom.

Abram was so much himself when he was praying about the fate of Sodom that he haggled with God like any Middle Eastern street trader. But even then, there was humility in his approach, for he argued his case on the basis of God's character:

> "Far be it from you to do such a thing — to kill the righteous with the wicked, treating the righteous and the wicked alike. Far be it from you! Will not the Judge of all the earth do right? . . . Now that I have been so bold as to speak to the Lord, though I am nothing but dust and ashes. . . . May the Lord not be angry, but let me speak just once more." (Genesis 18:25, 32)

When God tested the Patriarch over the sacrifice of Isaac, his words are the best anyone could speak when faced with such sacrifice: "Here I am," and "God will provide" (Genesis 22:1).

Moses' complaint was full-hearted and without guile: "O Lord, why have you brought trouble upon this people? Is this why you sent me?" (Exodus 5:22).

The familiarity in all these stories is that of loving son to loving father, rather than of one teenager to another. You feel that at any moment, the knees will bend and the head will bow and the mouth confess the sovereignty of God. These human cries are a reverent overflowing of emotion, and God in no way condemns them as long as they lead to an accepting prayer that begins to reach down into his will. Many of us have to face situations in which we find ourselves praying with Jesus, "Father, if possible, let this pass from me — nevertheless . . . nevertheless. . . ."

When the Apostles were released from their first imprisonment, as recorded in Acts 4, their prayer was rich in thoughts from their Scriptures, the Old Testament. It breaks down, verse by verse, into an excellent pattern. God is sovereign Lord (verse 24); God has spoken through David (verse 25); Jesus is the anointed Messiah (verses 26, 27); God is in control (verse 28); therefore strengthen us to speak, and express yourself here and now through the powerful name of Jesus (verses 29-30).

Another good pattern is found in the Old Testament in the prayer of Elijah before the priests of Baal. His main concern was the showing forth of the reality of God: "O Lord, God of Abraham, Isaac, and Israel, let it be known today [firstly] that you are God in Israel, [secondly] that I am your servant, and [thirdly] have done all these things at your command" (1 Kings 18:36).

In many of the Bible prayers, the immediate need is stated simply and briefly, as by a messenger who has returned from another country to report the situation to his king: "When the wine was gone, Jesus' mother said to him, 'They have no wine'" (John 2:3). Can you see the trust in her eyes?

St. Paul's prayers for the Christians at Philippi and Colossae are requests for discernment and righteousness to be given to them (Philippians 1:9-11, Colossians 1:9-

12). As with the other prayers in the Bible, they are definite and brief with a notable absence of fussing about details; sincerity is shown by simplicity rather than wordiness, but the qualities prayed for are all-embracing. You could pray for someone in this way for twenty years and, even if you had lost touch completely, you could know that the prayer remained right because it applies to any Christian at any time and place.

What matters is that we mean the words that we use

Some people who have been raised on formal prayers may suddenly discover how to speak to God as friend to friend, and in some cases the experience is so dramatic that they turn away from all set forms, to their own eventual impoverishment. Others, like me, work through a period in which only informality is taught, then weary of its limitation and begin to discover greater mental freedom in set forms.

Prewritten prayers, whether old or new, can be spoken as cold recitation — and spontaneity can degenerate into babbling self-indulgence. Either way, it is possible to use prayer-language to avoid God. When he comes too close — quick! throw some words into his face: something emotional by us or something beautiful by Cranmer. Maybe God will be satisfied and leave us alone. I am sometimes discouraged at how quickly I can react to the sound of his approaching feet. The gentlest drawing near on his part and I slam the door, "No, no! I came to prayer (or to church) to feel comfortable and comforted. Not this! My only petition is: Go away!"

In learning to deal with such defensiveness, we may find a slight change of prayer-language to be of help. It does not matter to God whether we address him in words that someone else has composed or in our own words. It *does* matter to him that we mean the words that we use. The question of which language style is better should be countered with another question: "Better for whom and better when?" It is a matter of usefulness and temperament. Extend your range like a climbing plant that stretches in several directions over the surface of a wall, following a way of prayer for however long it achieves its purpose. Prayer language is a means to an end, and that end is to know God.

✛   ✛

No authentic relationship between persons can exist without mutual freedom and spontaneity, and this is true in particular of inner prayer. There are no fixed and unvarying rules, necessarily imposed on all who seek to pray; and equally there is no mechanical technique, whether physical or mental, which can compel God to manifest his presence. His grace is conferred always as a free gift, and cannot be gained automatically by any method or technique. The encounter between God and man in the kingdom of the heart is therefore marked by an inexhaustible variety of patterns.

Bishop Kallistos of Diokleia,
The Power of the Name

Chapter 6

Structured Prayers

In literature and in everyday speech, words are repeated for stylistic emphasis or for emotional weight, and the same is true for the language of prayer. Unfortunately, the fear of "vain repetition" has made some Christians feel that they ought to pray spontaneously, year in and year out. At times of weariness, or tension, or great excitement, they may feel at a loss for words, but dare not shift their style to a set form, for fear of being like the Pharisees. In some denominations they may not even know a set form, except for the Lord's Prayer.

Though Jesus was against vainness (that is, emptiness) in prayer, he was not against repetition, and he said nothing against repeated words that were heartfelt. He told the story of a woman who changed the mind of an unjust judge by her continual coming with the same request. The point of the story is not that God is an unjust judge — the whole Bible teaches otherwise — but that the woman went on asking the judge for what she wanted, and eventually even an unjust judge relented (Luke 18:1-7). Jesus used repetition in Gethsemane when he prayed three times using the same words (Matthew 26:39-44).

The Old Testament contains examples of repetition that Jesus would have known well. He knew because, as God, he had inspired them and because, as a godly Jew, he had been taught the Hebrew Scriptures by his mother, his legal father, and the Rabbi in his village synagogue. In Psalm 118:1-4 and in all of Psalm 136 there is repetition that may or may not be empty, depending on how they are read. In our own lives we would be able to say, "His love endures for ever," or "Sing his praise, and exalt him for ever," many thousands of times and still not have exhausted the meaning.

Working with repetition

You may find it helpful to make your own spontaneous version of Psalm 136. Pray a short phrase — for example, "Thank you for the beauty of that tree," or "Show your love to this friend" — then follow it with the psalmist's words, "for your mercy endures forever." Then move to another short thought of praise or petition and follow it again with "for your mercy endures forever." Your own spontaneous words are in the first half of the prayer and the words of the psalmist are in the second.

No need for you to make up a new phrase every time; it depends on what you want to express. You may find yourself praying repeatedly for minutes on end, "Show your love to this friend, for your mercy endures forever; show your love to this friend, for your mercy endures forever; show your love. . . ."

None of this should be committed to paper, because it is a way of praying with the living flow of your thoughts. Take it slowly and you will find that a rhythm is set up in which your mind alternately roams widely in thankfulness or intercession and then is brought home to a single point of praise. Spontaneity and repetition balance each other, while the flow of thought is like the rhythm of breathing.

Another way to use repetition is to speak the name of Jesus three times and then follow it with a breath-length pause. Don't babble the name: you are speaking lovingly to someone who is there. The triple invocation "Jesus . . . Jesus . . . Jesus" draws the thoughts together as a number of loose pebbles are drawn up into a slowly closing hand, then your mind flies out with whatever thought is uppermost (what that thought is may surprise you sometimes). Then again pray "Jesus . . . Jesus . . . Jesus" and again express a breath-length thought of praise or petition or love. Provided you speak with respect, it may even be a thought of exasperation. I have had some terrible arguments with God, though of course I have lost every one.

This prayer has the opposite structure from the one based on Psalm 136, because in this case the repetition is in the first half and the spontaneity is in the second. As you synchronize it with your breathing, the spontaneous phrase will have to be breath-length and simple; it is good practice in concentrating and defining your thoughts with all your love or petition close-packed into the minimum of words. Expect to have to work with this for some time before it feels natural. Visualize the strong, controlled movement of an archer, the repeated Name "Jesus . . . Jesus . . . Jesus" being the bowstring drawn back and the short phrase flying forward as an arrow from heart to heaven. Sometimes you have no words to say; there is only a sigh.

. . . The Spirit helps us in our weakness. We do not know what we ought to pray for, but the Spirit himself intercedes for us with groans that words cannot express. And he who searches our hearts knows the mind of the Spirit, because the Spirit intercedes for the saints in accordance with God's will. (Romans 8:26, 27)

Patterns of words

Every set prayer is repeated in the sense that it has been said over and over by thousands of praying people over the centuries. Such prayers are neither so general in content as to be feeble, nor so up-to-date that in six months they will be out of date. An excellent structure is that used in the Collects of the Anglican Prayerbook. Here is the one for the 7th Sunday after Trinity Sunday:

Lord of all power and might, who art the author and giver of all good things; Graft in our hearts the love of thy Name, increase in us true religion, nourish us with all goodness, and of thy great mercy keep us in the same; through Jesus Christ our Lord.

Here is how it is shaped: 1. God is invoked with a title (Lord of all power and might); 2. He is addressed as acting in a certain way that is linked to that title (who art the author and giver of all good things); 3. He is asked for something that is linked to 1. and 2. (Graft . . . increase . . . nourish . . . keep). In this pattern, God is invoked, is described, and is petitioned.

Here is another Collect with the same structure, this time for the 23rd Sunday after Trinity:

> O God, our refuge and strength, who art the author of all godliness: Be ready, we beseech thee, to hear the devout prayers of thy Church; and grant that those things which we ask faithfully we may obtain effectually; through Jesus Christ our Lord.

If you find a form of words that expresses exactly what you want to say to God on a particular day, by all means say it as many times as you need to. The repetition becomes vain if you think it is the repetition that impresses God; or it becomes vain if your thoughts drift away to problems at the office or the pattern in the rug or the price of bacon, or anything irrelevant to the words you are saying. Whatever repeated words you use, do not babble; it would only make you breathless and tense. Even when you are repeating a short phrase to still the mind and to think around the words, some sweet content of the words should remain: otherwise, you might as well be repeating, "'Twas-brillig-and-the-slithy-toves-did-gyre-and-gimble-in-the-wabe."

Whether formal or informal, a prayer does not need to end with the words "in Jesus' name." It is not the form of words tagged onto the end that makes something a valid prayer: it is asking or praising according to God's mind and character and promises to us. Imagine that you have prayed for a neighbor, asking God to do something appallingly vindictive, then you end with the heartfelt words "in Jesus' name." No clear-thinking Christian would do such a thing. The name of Jesus represents all that he is; whether or not we use it explicitly, it stands as a sieve through which the words of all prayers must pass.

Give yourself time

A cure for babbling any set prayer is to go very slowly, and instead of looking directly at each phrase, to think over and around it, giving yourself time and mental elbowroom. This process of thought is different from trying to explain the phrase intellectually, or setting out statements of doctrine and cross-referencing to connected proof-texts. It is thinking in concepts rather than words, with your thoughts moving freely in the controlled environment of a single phrase, as though you were dancing within a circle of light. It takes practice to recognize when you are wandering too far.

It would be pointless to try to measure your progress by a standard of time, as though it were three times as spiritual to take half an hour over a prayer than to take only ten minutes. The purpose of going slowly is to do some fruitful thinking in and around the familiar phrases. Try exploring Psalm 92 or 139. Above all, give yourself time. In praying this way, you are setting your face against the shape, color, and tone of Western society; you are aiming for quality rather than speed, for depth rather than effect, and you are returning to roots and structures rather than following the lemmings over the clifftop that is signposted "New!"

The Psalms

The Psalms are the set prayers that stand above all others; everything you need to say to God is already said in them, and you can enter the psalmist's mind, thinking, "Where I am now, you have been; you spoke to our God from that place, now I will use your words and make them my own." The whole range of human emotions is there, including roars of imprecatory rage. Even though you may be troubled by the angry Psalms, you know there are times when we have to admit that we are part of the same human race that wrote them.

Among the riches of Christian prayers, the Scottish Presbyterian Church has given us the metrical version of the Psalms. While not every one is of equal poetic grace, singing them is easier for a congregation that is used to hymn tunes rather than plainchant. A verse of the metrical Psalms may be turned into a prayer for your private use, for example from Psalm 42:

> As pants the hart for cooling streams,
> When heated by the chase,
> So pants my soul for Thee, O Lord,
> And Thy refreshing grace.

Here is simple prayer from a Book of Hours, one of the books of private devotions used by the aristocratic laity in the late Middle Ages. The date of this one is 1514:

> God be in my heart, and in my understanding;
> God be in my eyes, and in my looking;
> God be in my mouth, and in my speaking;

God be in my heart, and in my thinking;
God be at my end, and at my departing.

Jesus knew and loved the Psalms and was familiar
with other Jewish prayers. As true man, he grew up as a
member of his society, and like other godly Jews he
would probably have memorized a long prayer called the
Eighteen Benedictions (also called *Amidah,* a word that
means "standing," because Jews stood to recite it). We
read that Jesus drew away from his disciples to pray
(Matthew 14:23); what would his words have been? He
would have spoken as a real human being and specifically
as a Jew.

Just as every Christian knows the Lord's Prayer, so
every Jew mentioned in the New Testament would have
known some version of the Eighteen Benedictions, parts
of which date from the 4th century B.C. Since it was so
well known to the first Christian disciples, it may have
been what was prayed in the upper room after the As-
cension, and by the first converts after Pentecost. In
times of great emotion, people return to the forms of
prayer that they know best, and what the Jewish Christians would have known as well as some of the Psalms
was the Eighteen Benedictions.

It is printed in full on pages 153-58. Enrich yourself
with such strong phrases from that ancient prayer as,
"Heal us, O Lord, and we shall be healed. . . . Save us,
and we shall be saved. . . ." Follow the pattern with your
own thoughts and needs, "Encourage me, O Lord, and
I shall be encouraged. . . . Humble me, and I shall be
humbled. . . ." Establish a verbal pattern and let your
prayers flow within it.

Memorizing

In our modern society we do not take kindly to having to memorize a prayer of over a thousand words; our minds have become lazy. But I know the value of some godly words committed to mind. When I was at school, we had to memorize the Apostles' Creed, the Ten Commandments, the Lord's Prayer, the Beatitudes, the *Magnificat,* the *Nunc Dimittis,* and the account of the Day of Pentecost in Acts 2:1-11; also the *Te Deum,* the General Thanksgiving, and the Collect for Peace from the Anglican *Book of Common Prayer.* As the homework assignments were handed out, month after month and term after term, we complained, of course, because it is the nature of schoolchildren to complain about homework. I now know that all that memorization did us no harm at all. We had to learn the words for the same simple reason that we had to learn the multiplication tables and the dates of the kings and queens of England from 1066 to 1952: the knowledge would be useful for us in life. I am not word perfect in the Bible passages or Collects, but when I hear them in church they feel thoroughly mine because I once had to learn them — as the splendid phrase has it — by heart.

Could you memorize a prayer of only eleven words? The Jesus Prayer has been familiar to Eastern Orthodox Christians since the 6th century. "Lord Jesus Christ, Son of the Father, have mercy upon us." Experiment with the rhythm of your breathing, whether a single breath in, then one out for the whole prayer, or the other way around. Breathe in with the words "Lord Jesus Christ, Son of the Father . . ."; breathe out with the words "have mercy upon us." Then again . . . and again, breath after breath.

The form of words is not absolutely fixed; you may say "Son of God" instead of "Son of the Father" or end with the words "have mercy" instead of "have mercy upon us." Take plenty of time finding out which rhythm feels best for you.

Here is another prayer from the Eastern Orthodox Church; it is a threefold invocation called the Trisagion:

> Holy God,
> Holy and strong,
> Holy and immortal
> Have mercy upon us.

If the rosary is part of the prayer tradition of your church, there is no reason why you couldn't say Jesus Prayers instead of Aves. As with all repeated forms, however, don't babble. The Jesus Prayer is not a mantra. The words have content, and they will take you to the Word himself; so *love* the words that you pray.

Feel free to use repetition and set forms of words in prayer. The Old Testament Jews did, and so did Jesus Christ, his disciples, the Apostles, the great Fathers of the church, and many thousands of Christians throughout all generations.

Structured prayer may be used as I suggested you use choreography: as something to help you to pray — if you find that it does help. A set prayer was never intended to be a substitute for the language of your own heart. Substituted for real prayer it would be as little use in learning to know God as would elaborate movements and positions performed for their own sake.

✝   ✝

The form of words makes no more difference to God than does the position you take. Pious phrases will not deceive or impress him for a moment, but the right words will be of immense help in learning to let tongue and heart speak the same language. A set prayer will express what you *want* to say, and will teach you to express what you *ought* to say. Prewritten words — like the discipline of time and place and position — are for your benefit, not his.

Chapter 7

Praying with an Outline

If you have been working through the suggestions in the previous chapters, then by this stage you have been praying by glances and silences throughout the day and have found a time and place that is best for you for regular prayer. You have been using movements and positions to help you and are discovering the balance between informal and structured language.

All this has been moving you from the more simple to the less simple, and from the general to the particular. Now that you have laid the groundwork, it is time to sort out the different parts of prayer. Think of four rooms labelled Intercession, Penitence, Praise, Reading. (Never mind about the working order for now; I have listed them alphabetically.)

Intercession includes praying for others, whether individuals or nations, friends and people you do not like or who may not like you. The key thought is: "He always lives to intercede for them" (Hebrews 7:25).

Penitence includes considering your own life, confession of sins great and small, receiving forgiveness, expressing sorrow for the sins of others, whether individuals or nations, and looking for the will of God. The key thought is: "Lord, have mercy upon us."

Praise includes general thanksgiving, particular thanksgiving for things in your own life, and thankfulness for God's work in other people's lives even though they themselves may not want to acknowledge it. The key thought is: "Delight yourself in the Lord" (Psalm 37:4).

The *Reading* may be a Psalm or another short passage from the Bible, something from a devotional book or a Collect or a hymn. The key thought is: "The unfolding of your words gives light" (Psalm 119:130).

Keep the four headings in mind and you will find that your thoughts will sort themselves out without strain. As to which of the four you start with on a particular day, this is so personal that no one should dictate it. You begin where you want to and move on from there. Some Christians say you must always begin with confession of sin, and that if you do not feel like it one day, you must be hiding something dreadful from God. It may be so. Equally it may be that, on that particular day, the chief thing in your mind is praise. So begin with praise if you want to and stay there as long as you wish. Prayer is a living relationship with a living God, and there is no one standing behind you ready to prompt you. The only two in that place of prayer are you and your Savior.

Now let's look at the four rooms in more detail (again, in alphabetical order).

Intercession

Since praying for others should not be at the mercy of your varying emotions from day to day, the best way to keep intercessions steady is to write the names down. All you need are names on a page, one to a line, with one or two words beside a few of them if you need help remembering the chief reason for praying. With most names you will not need any reminder.

Put down the date when you began to pray and decide how long to continue. When someone says to you, "Please pray for me," and you say, "Yes, of course," decide then and there whether to pray for a day, a week, a month, six months, or a year. You don't need to tell anyone; just decide within yourself. If there is an urgent need of prayer for someone on one day, you might decide to bring them before God every time the clock strikes, and if you are within the sound of a clock that chimes the quarter hours, so much the better. Intercession need be no more than a heartfelt glance to God with the person in mind.

Keep the list short and be willing to prune it from time to time, as you would be willing to prune an overgrown tree. It is better to pray regularly and properly for a few people than to rattle off name after name. I ease names off the list by moving them from the daily to the weekly one, because it feels less callous than simply crossing them out. Sometimes they ease themselves off, perhaps because the prayer has been answered or because someone else can pray for them better. God is the Master Craftsman who has many workers and apprentices in his workshop; he gives jobs to this one or that one, as he knows who can best do the work.

It is strange how a name sometimes stays stubbornly on your list for years. It doesn't seem to make much difference whether or not you are in touch with the person or even if you like them much. The one fact that has caught you and held you is that they need to be prayed for: you believe God has given you the job to do, so you do it.

Penitence

It is easy for this to become just a matter of liturgical conformity. In a congregation we say "we have sinned through our own most grievous fault," or words to that effect, but before God and alone, we tend to tell a different story. We tell him that what we did, said, or thought wasn't actually wrong, it was just that circumstances were against us on that day; we were tired; people like the ones we criticized always get on our nerves; keeping the Ten Commandments literally just isn't practical today; we were not raised as children to be any better; everyone nowadays does that kind of thing; no one cared; no one saw; no one knows; what we did or said wrong didn't matter anyway; the woman you gave to be with me, she gave me of the fruit; the serpent tricked me.

Just as there are no new sins, so there are no new excuses: God has heard them all. He knows every mitigating circumstance in the universe, and he has heard every conceivable excuse, both plausible and implausible. In the same way, an experienced teacher has heard every possible excuse for homework not having been done, and can evaluate every one.

It is because we *chose* to do wrong that we need to be forgiven, and a quiet, honest remembering will show that there was a moment — often a split second — of choice when we deliberately stepped onto the wrong path. If a particular choice is made enough times, that path becomes a well-trodden road that welcomes our feet. This is true both of bad and good choices: the ability lies in us to train our reactions. Of course there are times when God's mercy feels unreal, but it is fortunate that feelings do not indicate truth, in spite of what today's psycho-ridden Western society tells us. Pray for grace to be able to know God's forgiveness and to know that it is complete, whether you have the right feelings or not. Being able to forgive yourself is another matter; it is something that involves your wounded pride.

It is sometimes worth asking if you really want to have your guilt forgiven and taken away, or would choose to go on wallowing in remorse because it is a more familiar ache. There is great wisdom in the words of the Anglican General Confession, "forgive us all that is past." Be willing to lose face when you face God and to let what is past *be* past. Though we would often like to avoid the room called Penitence, it is sometimes the most blessed place to be in the whole world. Remember that on the days when you wish it were not there.

Let me tell you a true story. My nephew and his wife are missionaries in Japan; one of the people they had contact with was a man who had been a pilot in the Second World War. All members of the Japanese armed forces were trained to be brutal to the enemy because of the deeply held belief that to be of a defeated nation was the greatest shame. In a culture in which suicide was more honorable than surrender, the life of someone who

had surrendered was considered to be of no value. De-
cades later, when the elderly man wanted to become a
Christian, he could not understand how God could forgive him. Little by little he came to realize that the love
of God was greater than anything he had done.

Praise

Praise will grow with practice. No one can teach you
how to praise, any more than someone can teach you
how to love, but put yourself in the way of it again and
again, using praise-words that other people have written
until your own praise grows by itself. No need to try to
whip up your emotions to the pitch of the Hallelujah
Chorus: just begin where you are with simple gratitude.
Though praise is done deliberately, like walking through
a room, it will grow beyond a single room and become
a theme that accompanies you everywhere.

Reading

The Bible is on a different level from all other books:
God has inspired it, preserved it, and caused the church
to accept its unique authority for faith and practice. But
God also helps us through the whole fellowship of
Christian people who have spoken and written throughout all generations. When you pray, you are pressing
through yourself to know God better, and there may be
times when a Christian devotional book is more helpful
than the Bible; it can give you a new angle on things,
just as a Christian friend or pastor can.

I doubt if there is a devotional book in all the world of which anyone could agree with every word; even if you were to write your own, you would probably not agree with every word of it five or ten years later. However, here are eleven books that have proved their worth over many years and will continue to do so. The first was written more than fifteen hundred years ago, the most recent in 1995. It is unlikely that you will be equally attracted by each of them, so give yourself time to explore each book (maybe from a public library) before saying to yourself, "This is one that I can grow with."

(1) St. Augustine, *Confessions;* the spiritual diary of the 4th-century Bishop of Hippo in North Africa. When you read about some of his interior struggles, the intervening centuries fall away. (2) *The Cell of Self-knowledge: Early English Mystical Treatises by Margery Kempe and Others,* edited by John Griffiths. This is a gentle introduction to five writers who knew God centuries ago and whose advice is still relevant. One of them is Walter Hilton, who writes on prayer and hearing the angels' song. (3) and (4) Also from the late medieval period come two famous devotional books that are worth trying: *Revelations of Divine Love,* by Julian of Norwich, and the anonymous *Cloud of Unknowing.* (5) Thomas à Kempis's *The Imitation of Christ* is easily read pastoral wisdom, as fresh and relevant today as when it was written. (6) St. Francis de Sales, *Introduction to the Devout Life;* practical pastoral advice to an aristocratic lady from a 16th-century Bishop of Geneva. The writer was noted for Christian courtesy in an age of controversy. (7) *The Way of a Pilgrim* was written anonymously by an Orthodox monk in 19th-century Russia. He describes his discoveries as he learns to pray. (8) Thérèse of Lisieux's *History of a Soul*

is a spiritual diary of a middle-class French girl who was a Carmelite nun from the age of fifteen until her death nine years later. The theme is simplicity and obedience. (9) C. S. Lewis's *The Screwtape Letters,* written in 1942, are imaginary letters from a junior to a senior devil explaining how to tempt someone. It is illuminating to watch the process of temptation from the other side. (10) A. W. Tozer's *The Pursuit of God* is a 20th-century classic by an evangelical of wide Christian sympathy. (11) *Orthodox Lent, Holy Week & Easter,* by Hugh Wybrew; a good introduction to some of the verbal riches of the Orthodox tradition.

You will naturally be drawn towards a writer who thinks along the lines you already do and who seems like a friend. If a famous writer annoys you (as the ebullient Margery Kempe annoys me), try to find something in the words that you can learn from, then put that book aside for a while. A particular writer may not be for you now, and may never be; at least you won't have allowed yourself to toss the book across the room in complete rejection.

A lot of fruitful thinking can come from reading the Collects of the 1662 Anglican *Book of Common Prayer.* By all means go beyond your own church tradition, and don't be afraid; many people who have faithfully named the name of Christ have left a literary legacy that can enrich your prayers.

There are also modern books of newly written prayers, but I recommend that you stick to tried and tested devotional classics. As with pictures or music for worship, begin by nourishing your mind through the strong roots of Christian tradition. If, after a few years, modern words, sounds, or pictures enrich you, well and good. But whatever you read, now or later, the content of any devotional book must be tested by the teaching of the Bible.

If your reading is from the Bible, try a narrative passage. Most Bibles have paragraph headings so you know where one story begins and ends. Read the story again and again: watch it happening, seeing and feeling it as though you were present as the event unrolled around you. Feel the rough stone under your fingers and the early morning sun on your back as you lean down to peer into the empty tomb: be there.

As a brief guideline, ask yourself, "What did the people who were present think about this event?" Read the passage again, looking for the answer on the page. Ponder it for days if need be. Then ask yourself, "If I had been there, what would I have thought?" This time the answer is not on the page: it is in your heart. Take as long as you like with the questions, being as honest as you dare. Keep the second question in mind and ask, "Why would I have thought like that?" The final question is, "What practical difference will I let it make in my life in the next twenty-four hours?" These questions bring a biblical narrative gently towards you, from history to head, to heart, to hand. Of the Gospels, St. Luke's is especially good for this kind of reading.

When you read a passage that you can't understand, don't panic or turn to a commentary or cross-references. Books of explanation are not for your praying time. Look through the passage again and find something that you do understand, however slight it may be, and consider how to put that slight knowledge into practice in the following days.

A single story can give you enough food for thought

for days, and you don't have to go through a Gospel from beginning to end. At first you may want to read a new passage every day, dashing through every question and taking mental notes with one eye on the clock. In time you will find more than you thought possible without moving on. There is no required time because this is a matter of growing and perceiving. We have to learn to do things at God's speed.

Chapter 8

Being a Go-between

People pray for one another because they believe it makes a difference: that is what undergirds intercession. The wish to do it is so natural that it is often the first thought in the mind of a new convert; as soon as the heart quickens with God's life, it turns towards others. Then we learn to bring people to God, one by one, year after year, and we learn to continue even though there may be no visible result. To intercede means to go between, and it is holy work. Christ always lives to make intercession for us, so when we pray for someone else, we are joining in his work.

If praying for someone else is an unfamiliar exercise, bring one person to mind as needing to know the love of God, express within yourself "if only," and dare to feel it as strongly as you can. Then gently and firmly turn that phrase towards God's face and hold it there. Intercession need not involve many words or it may become a fantasy scenario of someone else's life. The plain fact is that while we don't know what is best for that person, God does; to pray only, "Your will be done," seems at first to be a way of opting out, but to pray it thoughtfully becomes more strenuous all the time. We don't know what it would take for someone to know God better: it might be being in an airplane wreck and losing a limb. When we ask for God's will, we must realize that it could mean disaster, humanly speaking. If you can look back at a time of great difficulty which, in spite of everything, drew you nearer to God, you can see things from a different perspective. No one would have wished the difficulty onto you, but now you are glad that things happened the way they did.

The word "Father" can obscure our relationship with God if we use it to reduce the sense of his majesty so we can feel snug in his presence. We must become aware of the dark, dazzling hugeness of God; we bring our plans to him as a candle is held up to the sun or a cup of water carried to a sparkling spring. How would we dare to ask for anything outside his will?

Listen to St. Augustine in his *Confessions:*

> You, God, who alone are good, have never ceased to do good. Some indeed of our works are good through Your grace, but they are not eternal: after them we hope that we shall first find rest in the greatness of Your sanctification. But You, the Good, who need no good besides, are ever in repose. What man will give another man the understanding of this, or what angel will give another angel, or what angel give a man? Of You we must ask, in You we must ask, at You we must knock. Thus only shall we receive, thus shall we find, thus will it be opened to us.

Listen to Job, howling in his bereavement: "May the Name of the Lord be praised" (Job 1:21).

Does God do his will in a life, regardless of whether or not we ask for it? This is the catch-22 of Christian prayer. We all have to live with it, poised between fatalism and panic: fatalism that God will do his will regardless of what we pray for, and panic that he is tied hand and foot unless we are on our knees. No weight of Bible verses can tip the scales one way or the other because the Bible presents both sides, and precisely in the middle comes the prayer, "Your will be done." We choose his will by an act of our will, and by choosing it we become part of his activity in the world.

Thirteen years ago my prayer list included the names of a parish priest, a singer, an editor, a suburban mother, an El Salvadorian teenager, and a Catholic nun. Now there is the monarchy, another priest and another editor, the same singer, a doctor, and a little girl that I saw begging in Istanbul. Though their needs are as different as their lives, their needs resolve into one: that all things belonging to the Spirit may live and grow in them. It is as though we had handed God a piece of paper bearing someone's name and a dotted line for him to fill in.

This kind of intercession is disturbingly open-ended; we would love to write our own ideas on that line, we could fill it with the most interesting plans. Instead, we hand God the unmarked paper, knowing that he knows best. Taking one name at a time, picture yourself raising it with the gesture of a child who holds something up for the attention of a trusted adult. The only word of the child is, "Look." It may help you to perform that movement very slowly with both hands.

It is not that God needs our gesture but that we express something better when we do it with more than one part of ourselves. In Old Testament worship, incense was not needed to take prayers to God, but the sight and fragrance of incense was a picture to help the worshippers.

Great benedictions and intercessions in the Bible can be made personal by adding a friend's name and saying "him" or "her" as the case may be.

The Lord bless ——— and keep [———]; the Lord make his face to shine upon ——— and be gracious unto [———]; the Lord lift up the light of his countenance upon ——— and give [———] peace. (Numbers 6:24-26, King James Version)

This is my prayer: that ———'s love may abound more and more in knowledge and depth of insight, so that [———] may be able to discern what is best and may be pure and blameless until the day of Christ, filled with the fruit of righteousness that comes through Jesus Christ — to the glory and praise of God. (Philippians 1:9-11)

Fill ——— with the knowledge of God's will through all spiritual wisdom and understanding . . . that [———] may live a life worthy of the Lord and may please him in every way: bearing fruit in every good work, growing in the knowledge of God, being strengthened with all power according to his glorious might so that [———] may have great endurance and patience, and joyfully give thanks. . . . (Colossians 1:9-12)

I always thank my God as I remember ——— in my prayers, because I hear about [———'s] faith in the

Lord Jesus and [————'s] love for all the saints. I pray that ———— may be active in sharing [————'s] faith, so that [————] will have a full understanding of every good thing we have in Christ. (Philemon 4-7)

May the God of peace, who through the blood of the eternal covenant brought back from the dead our Lord Jesus, that great Shepherd of the sheep, equip ———— with everything good for the doing of his will, and may he work in ———— what is pleasing to him, through Jesus Christ, to whom be glory for ever and ever. Amen. (Hebrews 13:20-21)

To him who is able to keep ———— from falling and to present [————] before his glorious presence without fault and with great joy — to the only God our Savior be glory, majesty, power and authority, through Jesus Christ our Lord, before all ages, now and for evermore! Amen. (Jude 24-25)

You can pray the Jesus Prayer or the Trisagion (Chapter 6) as an intercession, fixing someone in your attention and beaming the Jesus Prayer in that person's direction like a beam of powerful healing light. You may find it helpful to put the person's name into the prayer: ". . . have mercy upon ———— ." When you pray like that, your little requests are measured against the great words of the Bible and the church. It will help you to develop a larger language in your own informal prayers.

Unspecific but clearly focussed

Though there are times when we would like to ask that God make his will so clear to someone that that person could not doubt in which direction to go, this may be too specific a request. The person may need to walk by faith rather than by unmistakable leading, however exciting that leading may be. I remember a friend's telling me, "I'm praying that there will be a light at the end of your tunnel." The request was unspecific but clearly focussed. The greatest thing we can do for people is to bear them into the rich presence of God and hold them there: no words are needed. Holding someone before God, steadily, steadily, steadily while the seconds tick by, is different from fond musing about an absent friend: it is positive and active, done with the will. Look at God and hold that person before his face. You will soon discover that prayer is work.

I have found that praying for someone without being too specific eliminates pride. You ask that a woman turn towards God, or that a man begin to acknowledge the love of Christ in his difficult life. There is no dictating to God how it should happen, so there can be no bragging to your friends, "Oh yes, *I* prayed for her to find a Christian husband in six months!" or "*I* was the one who asked God to send that $500 for the mission fund!" Jesus had sharp words about people who did their prayers or acts of almsgiving before an audience. He said that they have their reward, and he was right, of course: their reward is the praise of their friends. It is better just to pray and be quiet about it; then if there is an answer all you can feel is, "This is the Lord's doing, and it is wonderful in our eyes" (Psalm 118:24).

Do not baptize gossip

It is remarkable how little you need to know about people in order to pray for them. A lot of information can be distracting because it parades facts and opinions before your mind when you want to concentrate on bringing the person to God. Gossip is a terrible thing anywhere, any-time, and especially in the phrase, "I'm only telling you this so you can pray about it!" Intercession develops com-passion, and compassion prays but doesn't pry.

Wordless heaviness

On very rare occasions you may be given to feel a deep heaviness. Bear it in silence: you are being asked to share the weight of someone else's sorrow or pain or worry, though this person may not be aware at the time of having been prayed for. This heaviness is different from ordinary human sorrow and has an unmistakable given-ness. It may take you by surprise. You can no more make it happen than you can make the lightning flash. This heaviness is not an indication that you should stop pray-ing, but is a sign that a different quality of intercession has just begun. If you pray for someone only when it feels pleasant, what profit is that?

Praying for someone you fancy

If you are sexually attracted to someone who is not yours, don't pray for that person at all. Fallen human nature has an amazing way of trying to baptize its sin. You may know without question that it is wrong to let your thoughts dwell on someone, so you try to put that person out of your mind. Can you pray for the person? Oh yes, of course, you tell yourself, you can do that with impunity; and in the great name of Intercession you let your mind take its ease where it has no right to be. Since you can't do it without spiritual danger, don't do it at all. Trust God that other people will pray for that person: as for you, close the door and do not let that name come before you again.

Praying for someone you dislike

If there is someone you dislike, put that name on your prayer list at once and keep it there. At first you will feel like the greatest hypocrite in the world, praying fiercely and with emotions like those in the angry Psalms. Knowing that a particular name is on your prayer list, you will find a dozen reasons for avoiding prayer altogether. As you lift the name before God day after day, all you can see is the fact that you have been wronged, or that you dislike the person, but pray anyway. Repeat the Lord's Prayer and do not give up, even though one of the phrases will stick in your throat.

In time you will begin to think less with your own mind and more with what must be the mind of Christ. At first you won't want to do any of this because you enjoy hating someone; it raises you in your own estimation and gives you an inner force that drives you through the day with your head high. It is only when you begin to dissolve dislike by prayer that you make an unpleasant discovery about yourself: in certain situations and with certain people, you like to hate.

Jesus said, "Love your enemies and pray for those who despitefully use you." We are *commanded* to pray for our enemies, and that includes praying for someone we merely dislike. Love is too important to be left to the emotions: it must be made an act of the will. When you obey Christ's order literally, you will find that wonderful things will happen. So if there are people you hate, pray for them every day until they become people you love.

Praying for a nation

When you pray for a town, neighborhood, or nation, find out what you can about it. Missionary letters will give only a partial view: you can get additional information from your local library. Get to know the country, its history and national character; then you can pray with understanding. If it is mentioned in the media, you will find a personal interest pricking up your ears. It is no longer just an area of industrial wasteland, or a place somewhere in Africa that has received a new name. It belongs to you now because you have loved it before God. Whether or not you might like living there is ir- relevant: prayer forges a stronger relationship.

When you think of other countries, be thankful for modern communications. When America was estab- lished, it took many weeks for a letter to travel between England and America. That span of time had an effect on 18th-century politics because the colonies felt very far away to people on both sides of the Atlantic. Today, when business communications can zip around the world by fax or e-mail, prayer requests can travel the same way.

Commending to God people
who have died

This is something that not every Christian feels at ease
with. If you are one of those, remember the great age of
the practice and consider this prayer from the Jewish
memorial service, putting your friend's name in it:

> God full of compassion whose presence is over us,
> grant perfect rest beneath the shelter of your presence
> with the holy and pure on high who shine as the lights
> of heaven, to ——— who has gone to his everlasting
> home. Master of mercy, cover him in the shelter of
> your wings forever, and bind his soul into the gather-
> ing of life. It is the Lord who is his heritage. May he
> be at peace in his place of rest. Amen. (*Forms of Prayer
> for Jewish Worship;* The Reform Synagogues of Great
> Britain, 1977)

Here is a prayer from the 4th century, by Serapion,
Bishop of Thmuis in Egypt:

> O God, who hast authority of life and death, God of
> the spirits and Master of all flesh, God who killest
> and makest alive, who bringest down to the gates of
> Hades and bringest up, who createst the spirit of man
> within him and takest to thyself the souls of the saints
> and givest rest, who alterest and changest and trans-
> formest thy creatures, as is right and expedient, being
> thyself alone incorruptible, unalterable and eternal.
> We beseech thee for the repose and rest of this thy
> servant; give rest to his soul, his spirit, in green places,

in chambers of rest with Abraham and Isaac and Jacob and all thy saints: and raise up his body in the day which thou hast ordained, according to thy promises which cannot lie, that thou mayst render to it also the heritage of which it is worthy in thy holy pastures. Remember not his transgressions and sins and cause his going forth to be peaceable and blessed. Heal the grief of his relatives who survive him with the spirit of consolation, and grant unto us all a good end, through the only begotton Son, Jesus Christ, through whom with thee is the glory and the strength in the Holy Spirit for ever and ever. Amen.

Isn't that lovely? ". . . give rest to his soul, his spirit, in green places. . . ."

Dead people are not lost like lost car keys; they have not been snuffed out like a candle flame. We know exactly where they are: they are in God's hands, as is the whole world in one way or another. A funeral and a proper period of grieving (both of which are grossly undervalued processes of emotional healing in Western society) are ways of bringing a friendship in this world to a decent end. When someone we love dies, our love for that person continues, even though we do not try to get in touch. Our loss and grief are real. We may need to commend that soul to God's hands many times before we are free to enjoy the good memories, and to live in a world in which that person no longer is. There will be renewed friendships in heaven. Till then we release the person into the hands of the judge of all the earth.

If prayer is limited to asking for things like a better job or for financial help, it is obviously foolish to pray for dead friends because they live beyond such things. It is as hard for us to imagine that life as it is for a pre-born child to imagine life outside the womb. Once you begin to enlarge prayer to include Numbers 6:24-26, the picture changes: "May the Lord make his face to shine upon him." If you have ever walked away from a friend's grave thinking confusedly, "I hope he's happy," you have expressed a prayer for the dead in its simplest form. This spontaneous reaction has been part of Christian experience for two thousand years.

The most charming prayer for the dead is this one: "May God grant him more than he deserves." At first you smile — then you think, "Yes: that's grace!"

Praying when you should do something else as well

"Suppose a brother or sister is without clothes and daily food. If one of you says to him, 'Go, I wish you well; keep warm and well fed,' but does nothing about his physical needs, what good is that?" (James 2:14-17). To say "There, there, I'll pray for you" is a mockery if what is needed is action as well as words.

Let me tell you a true story. When our teenage son was in the hospital seriously injured, I was back in the house, trying to keep daily life ticking over, my mind in suspended animation with worry. There was a ring at the door, and I opened it to see a member of my congregation. She put a tuna casserole into my hands, saying, "There's your supper," and then she turned and went down the front path. I knew her well and I knew she was praying for us, but she understood that she shouldn't *only* pray.

A few days later the doorbell rang again; this time it was an elderly next-door neighbor. She strode into the wreck of the kitchen, announcing, "I've come to do the dishes." My husband, daughter, and I were so dazed with distress that we just stood and watched her do it. When the job was finished, she hung up the apron, said, "There you are," then walked out. Those simple acts of kindness have glowed in my memory for years.

It is all too easy to use the promise of prayer as an excuse for avoiding doing something else as well: a meal cooked and presented, small children cared for, help with the laundry. "I'll come tomorrow morning when you've had time to think, and you can give me a shopping list," or "I've called two mothers whom your children know well, to do your school run." If you hear that an elderly person's dog or cat has died, recognize it as a serious bereavement, and then think, "Does he have the strength to dig the grave, or will he have to put the dead pet out with the trash?" Don't just pray: find a spade and get on the phone. When you hear that someone has lost her job, recognize it as a career bereavement, then think, "Do I have a business contact who may have a practical idea?" Modern communications can open possibilities. Don't just pray: get on the phone or the internet.

To intercede means to go between, and it is holy work. Christ always lives to make intercession for us, so when we pray for someone else, we are joining in his work.

✛   ✛

Your love, Jesus, is an ocean with no shore to
bound it; and if I plunge into it, I carry with me
all the possessions I have. You know, Lord, what
those possessions are — the souls you have seen
fit to link with mine.

St. Térèse of Lisieux

Chapter 9

Praying without Words

It is easy to say "when words fail," as though words were the only legitimate way of praying and all other ways were suspect or of a lesser order of reality. The weakness of the Protestant tradition is that it tends to limit worship to words, undervaluing other means of expression; this is a profound misunderstanding of how people behave.

In everyday life there are times of joy when words are not enough and when feelings are better expressed with a smile or a hop or a hug or some joyful sound. Prayer is sometimes the same; all you can do is exist, breathe, and praise. At other times you may be anxious for someone but have no words to express it. Never mind. Hold that person up and look at God without trying to say anything. (Note: look at God, not at the person you are holding up.)

Don't be afraid of your senses

C. S. Lewis wrote, "God likes matter, he invented it," and in those six words he summed up the theology of the

Incarnation. Because Christianity is an incarnational religion, we do not need to be afraid of the material world of
taste and scent and sound and touch and movement and
sight. We do not need to be afraid of matter, and if we
believe the credal statements about the Creation and the
Incarnation, we are wrong if we try to escape it.

What a pity that the word "sensual" has become
infected with the idea of sexual lust, though the basic
meaning of the word is "of the physical senses." There
is an inescapable physicality in Christian prayer and worship; it involves unspoken words formed in the mind by
a complex process that not even neurologists claim to
understand; there are words spoken with the tongue and
the larynx; there is music produced by controlled breath,
and instruments that make sound; there are limbs that
walk, sit, kneel, bow, and trace the shape of the cross;
there are taste buds that receive the dissolving texture of
the Sacrament, eyes that see and ears that hear, noses that
smell fresh flowers and furniture polish and (in some
churches) incense and beeswax candles.

The medieval Cathars, who professed an angelic
Christ who did not really undergo human birth and
death, preached a lifestyle that tried to deny the reality
of the material world. These ascetics forbade marriage,
meat, and dairy food, and taught that matter was created
by the Devil, that what was invisible was pure, and that
everything we could see was intrinsically evil. But the
Bible begins with the words, ". . . God created the
heavens and the earth . . . ," and in the Nicene Creed,
we say that we believe God created all things visible and
invisible: let's hold to that truth and not slip into becoming closet Cathars — or join any other group that says
materiality is evil.

Consider that all wood and metal are special now because the Cross was made of wood and nails, that all water is special now because Christ was baptized in it, that all the ground is special now because he walked on it, and so on with every physical part of the world we live in. Rather than being evil, the material world, which includes our senses, is part of what our good God has made. Although it has been wrenched by the Fall, like a limb out of joint, the Incarnation took place in it and has changed it forever.

God warned his people about the misuse of physical objects, but true worship was not compromised by the carved cherubim on either side of the ark, nor by the lions, cherubim, and bulls that were carved or embroidered on other articles in the Temple (Exodus 37 and 1 Kings 7).

The sense of sight

Sight has been used in godly worship from the beginning. The Old Testament is filled with pictorial object lessons: the garments of skin made by God for Adam and Eve, the lamb offered by Abel, the Temple adorned with sculpture, metalwork, spinning, dyeing, and weaving. The sense of sight has been in Christian worship from a simple picture of the Virgin and Child with a star in early Christian art, to the windows of Chartres Cathedral ablaze with light, and on to some of the better examples of visual art in modern churches.

Medieval Christians valued sight as the highest of the senses because it is connected with light, and God is light; that is why they brought light into their places of worship, filtering it through glass pictures that showed his glory. Before Gothic architecture with walls of light-transmitting glass, there was an expanse of solid walls that were bright with pictures. Worshippers saw the Old Testament prophets, guardian angels, and events from the Gospels; every time they went into their church they watched saints and sinners being divided as sheep from goats at the Last Judgment. Those pictures stayed in their minds and hearts to correct, to guide, and to warn.

Not everyone has understood the power and glory of the sense of sight in Christian worship. I could give many examples of those who didn't; the following is a description of how Protestants behaved in Bayeux Cathedral one day in May 1562. The description is based on eyewitness reports and on comparison of an earlier inventory with what remained after that day. Armed men burst into the cathedral and to the sound of a drumbeat "they broke, demolished, and overthrew statues, coffers, benches, tables, seats, doors, windows, locks, hinges, paintings, and iron railings; grasped, broke, ripped, burned, looted, and carried away a great number of copes, chasubles, tunics, and dalmatics, chalices, jewels, silverwork, linens and other things that serve in the celebration of the Holy Liturgy."

There are well-documented examples of such behavior across the Western world from Constantinople to Scotland, many of them in the countries of Northern Europe during the Protestant Reformation. Instead of a reasoned, courteous response to some cases of idolatry, irrational rage was poured out against every inanimate object in the cathedral, including chairs, tables, and hinges. Mindless vandalism is a skeleton in the Protestant closet.

But though people of that mind-set have left their mark in destruction, they are in a minority among God's people. Through two thousand years, most Christians have avoided idolatry while not being afraid of beautiful things as an aid to prayer: they have understood and acted on the truth that is well expressed in six words: "God likes matter, he invented it."

Praying with pictures

Before the 8th century and from the 9th century to today, Eastern Orthodox churches have contained special pictures, or icons, of Christ, the Virgin, the saints, and scenes from the Old and New Testaments. Orthodox Christians reverence their icons as doorways to the world of the spirit, believing that honor paid to them is honor paid to their prototypes. Does it lead to idolatry? I have never met anyone who confused a picture with the person whose picture it is. It is likely that you have a picture of a beloved relative or friend in your house, but I doubt that you would confuse it with the living person. I also doubt that you would throw it down and stamp on it.

The honor that Orthodox Christians pay to an icon passes through the physical medium of the picture to the heavenly reality. They look towards an icon when they pray, believing that it is a door — no more, no less. You may find that an icon helps you to pray by being a door, or simply as a means of focussing your eyes and your mind. If you come to find that it is a help, you will be joining millions of God's people who are not afraid of the sense of sight.

An icon can be made of any non-ephemeral medium. It can be a low-relief carving in ivory or gemstones, or made of mosaic, metal, tiles, paint, weaving or a piece of embroidery or knitting. What makes it an icon is its style, a way of presenting the great people and events of Christianity that is above art fashion and is therefore never going to look out of date. It is not meant to be a realistic picture like something seen through a camera lens, because it is more important than that; it shows the spiritual reality as well as the outer aspect. Some icons have several events of Old or New Testament history in one picture, because the whole event is important; some dispense with background and show a saint standing on tiptoe against a sheet of gold, because he is living in the light of God. Icons never show God except as Incarnate Son.

Your eyes may have become satiated with 19th-century Western religious art (often sentimental) or with late 20th-century religious art (often aggressive and jagged). Instead, just to whet your appetite and give you a sense for what resources are available, I am presenting at the end of this chapter five icons from the hundreds of possibilities. Though there are good pictures from later than the 16th century, I have chosen earlier ones that take you back to the strong roots of Christian art. Begin there, to define and inform your taste. Later, you may want to explore the work of later painters or sculptors whose work is well rooted, such as Memling, El Greco, Rouault, and Epstein.

Christianity has developed through the guidance of the Holy Spirit for two thousand years, and for most of those years and in most nations where Christians have lived and prayed, pictures have been a normal part of worship. What is new and alien to incarnational worship is the *insistence* on plain walls, shut eyes, rigid limbs, everyday language, and the absence of color, scent, and symbol.

Using music

If there is an occasion when words of prayer are not possible, you can use music, letting it speak for you in an active process in which your face is open towards God. Keep your attention on him, listening *through* the music rather than *to* it, using it as communication.

You can choose from a wide range of classics and 20th-century music, such as César Franck's setting of *Panis angelicus,* or "Worthy Is the Lamb" from Handel's *Messiah,* or hymn settings by John Rutter, or Paul McCartney's *Let It Be,* or *Canto Gregorianum,* a recent recording of plainchant by Spanish monks. For music without words, try the Adagio from Mozart's *Clarinet Concerto in A-major,* or Samuel Barber's *Adagio for Strings* (the music need not be explicitly Christian or even religious), or John Tavener's *The Protecting Veil.* For simple joy, smile at God and play Charlie Parker's *Birdland* or Ralph Vaughan Williams's *The Lark Ascending.* Unless you are musically trained, short pieces would probably be best. John Tavener (an Orthodox Christian) is an acquired taste for ears used to Western classical music, but a taste well worth acquiring.

God has given you ears, eyes, and limbs, a nose, a tongue, and a sense of touch: use them and rejoice.

Using silence

There are small moments between glancing prayers that are filled with a sweet absence of words. Practice extending those moments by a few seconds until silence is familiar territory. It is not the awkward silence of having nothing to say, or a pause for breath while you fantasize an "answer." The silence I mean is full and rich and positive. The phrase that the Quakers use is "centering down."

There will be times when words fail through weariness or because you have brought a problem to God many times before. Don't strain to say anything, but put aside even the thought of words; bring to God the weariness that you feel and let that offering *be* the prayer, knowing that he hears a sigh as clearly as he hears words. Remember that you can let a position speak for you. Silence before God is like silence in the presence of a good friend.

The psalmist said, "As the eyes of slaves look to the hand of their master, as the eyes of a maid look to the hand of her mistress, so our eyes look to the Lord our God, till he shows us his mercy" (Psalm 123:2).

The nearest to that in our society is a well-trained dog whose joy in life is to be the servant of its handler. A police dog, sheepdog, or seeing-eye dog shows its devotion in every movement of its eyes. It loves to be beside its master, frequently looking into his face, as alert and relaxed as only a happy and useful dog can be. The least order is obeyed instantly, and when there is no order the dog's chief delight is to be beside its master in love and silence.

If the psalmist had written in the 20th or 21st century, he might have said, "As the eyes of a well-trained dog look to the hand of its master. . . ." So explore silence: wordiness in prayer is like incessant barking.

Tongues

This is praying without words in the sense that the words are not understood without translation. The Apostle Paul was firm with the Corinthian congregation. He told the speakers in tongues that no more than three should exercise their gift during public worship, that they should wait for one another, and that there should always be translation. He expected the gift of tongues to be under the control of the will, because the speakers had to wait for one another and they had to forgo speaking if three had already spoken. If there was no translator, they had to be quiet (1 Corinthians 14:26-40).

Some Christians are given the ability to speak in strange words when they pray. The sound is a soft murmuring or whispering with an occasionally recognizable ". . . Jesus . . . Jesus. . . ." Singing in tongues is the same thing in musical form, in which more than one person repeats short musical phrases that blend together. The effect is gentle and beautiful. I said that some are given the ability: God gives where he chooses, though some Christians, through pride or spiritual jealousy or just plain muddleheadedness, try to grasp what they have not been given. The famous love chapter, 1 Corinthians 13, is part of St. Paul's stern warning to a congregation whose tongues of men and angels were causing trouble. It is not for us to snatch gifts from one another like children on Christmas morning. Whether you have the gift of tongues or not, the basics of prayer are the same, and they are unexciting: a discipline of time and place, a balance of praise, humility, intercession, and tuning a life to God's will. There is enough in those basics to last a lifetime.

In the 14th century, Walter Hinton wrote to a friend about hearing the song of angels:

> If you introduce presumption into your imagination and actions, and so become prey to disordered fantasies, like mad people, without the ordering of the mind that grace brings, and without the support of spiritual strength, then the way is open for the devil to come into your soul and deceive you with his false enlightenment, false sounds and false comforts. A soul then becomes the false ground in which error and heresy can flourish, along with false prophecy, presumption and false reasoning, blasphemy, slander and a load of other evils.

Though Hinton doesn't deny that angels can be heard, notice his careful phrase "the ordering of the mind that grace brings."

Fasting

"I thank God that I am not as other men," prayed the Pharisee, "I fast twice a week." Most of us thank God that we are not like that Pharisee: we don't fast at all.

In some parts of the church the silence on the subject of fasting is deafening. In nearly two thousand sermons, of which about half were evangelical, I have yet to hear a single one on the subject of fasting. The reasons the ancient discipline is not popular today may be a fear of doing a good work to earn credit with God and a failure to understand that it is flesh and blood that prays. Add to that the effect of today's cult of softness and it is not hard to see why fasting is thought to belong in a spiritual museum along with whips and hairshirts. Every society begins Stoic and ends Epicurean. I grew up in a house without central heating or double glazing, in a village without street lighting, and though I could still live in such a house today, I'd prefer not to have to; one generation's luxury becomes the next generation's normal standard of life.

In other centuries a fast was not an excuse either to trim the waistline or to save money, but was a positive opportunity to strengthen the soul. Today you and I are bombarded with propaganda that tells us to be physically at ease every waking moment. Comfortable clothes, warm houses, convenient transportation, beds, and good food are considered normal — so normal that if we are deprived of any of them, we squeal like a piglet lifted away from its trough.

Everyday life was once a lot tougher, and a Lenten discipline was tougher still: there were whips and hairshirts, crusts and water, and kneeling on stone floors half the night. Today we are unwilling to give up sugar on cornflakes. If we are not going to save money or lose weight by fasting, we say, "What is the point?" The point is that if it were only the soul that spoke to God, the body could be in any state consistent with good stewardship (that is, neither drunk, drugged, tranquilized, hung over, nor overfed). To let the stomach stay empty in order to pray better makes sense because there is a unity between body and soul.

The Old Testament Prophets denounced the misuse of fasting: we need to rediscover its use. By the 1st century it was an accepted part of good Jewish life with a twice-weekly abstention from wine and meat. By saying "When you fast," rather than "if," Jesus was taking the practice for granted and was making sure his disciples had their motives right before they continued. We need to get our motives right before we begin.

Though we usually think of fasting with reference to food, there are other ways to fast. Married people have their own way of denying themselves legitimate pleasure for the sake of something more important (1 Corinthians 7:5). Tithing is a form of fasting, the giving up of something that is not bad in itself because it is the *love* of money that is the root of all evil. Whatever form of fasting you choose, give up something that affects your soft life. To "try" to go without sugar in tea "for a few weeks" is a vague plan that is likely to be forgotten before it has really begun; moreover, it comes too close to being a slimming diet. Instead, plan to give up one thing in your life from one calendar date to another, and do it to discipline yourself in prayer for a friend's salvation. Fasting is a positive act; you do it in a definite way, for a definite time, and for a definite reason.

Now the hard part: don't talk about it. Plan a fast that you can keep to with a minimum of social fuss. Having to explain to people why you are not eating or drinking this or that is a fine way to spiritual pride. You are responsible to your employer for doing a good day's work, so don't undertake more than you can cope with. Though you will have days when you don't want to pray at all and must take yourself by the scruff of the neck to do it, if your chosen fast is making you heartsick, you have attempted too much. Apologize to God and simplify till you have found a workable plan. You are relating yourself to him, not to another Christian who may be older and tougher.

Fasting is praying without words. When your body craves whatever it is that you have chosen to do without, turn that craving into a prayer for something or someone. The turning movement of the mind is conscious and deliberate like redirecting a spotlight. As long as you want what you have chosen to say no to, the prayer continues without words.

✣   ✣

It is wise to ask yourself from time to time, "Why do I want to pray better?" If the main purpose is to achieve internal quietness, you are looking for a nice religious feeling rather than contact with the dangerous, living Christ. We use movements and positions and music and pictures to speak for us because they are as much a part of our created world as grammar and syntax.

Fig. 1 Detail of *Virgin and Child Hodegitria,* 14th century, School of Constantinople, now in the Byzantine Museum, Athens. This iconic type of the Virgin and Child is called *Hodegitria* (accent on the third syllable), a Greek word that means "someone who shows the Way." Both figures look at you out of the picture. Christ's hand is raised in blessing as he sits enthroned on the Virgin's left arm, and he holds a scroll that symbolizes his divine wisdom. In medieval art the faces are still but the hands speak. Look at the Virgin's left hand: it directs your attention to the Child. This icon is not a poster telling you to go to Mary with your troubles; instead, she looks directly at you and says, "Do whatever he tells you." Three created beings are looking at them: the archangels Michael and Gabriel in heaven and you on earth. *The Virgin Hodegetria 14 century, Athens. Byzantine Museum T.177. Courtesy of the Byzantine Musuem.*

Fig. 2 *The Holy Face,* Novgorod, 1500, now in the National-almuseum, Stockholm. The small size of this icon indicates that it was made for private devotional use, a loved picture on the wall of someone's home as a conduit for daily prayers nearly five centuries ago. Of course, you are not praying to a picture — who would be so silly as to think so? You are praying towards a representation of Jesus Christ; you are a physical person speaking *through* a material object, *to* the Incarnate. There are many examples of Holy Face icons with small variations of hair and a background. I like this one because Christ looks as though he is listening. *Courtesy of the Swedish National Museums.*

Fig. 3 *St. George and the Dragon,* Novgorod, 15th century, now in the Russian Museum, Moscow. As you can see from the horse's back legs, this is not meant to be a real animal; it shows the spiritual control of the soldier saint who disciplines his life by the grace of God the way a rider controls a powerful horse. The dragon coils out of a dark cave under hills topped with dancing rocks that proclaim God's victory. The hand of God blesses the saint from the top corner of the icon, in a segment of a circle that represents the whole sphere of heaven. The lance is a spiritual weapon rather than a real implement of cold steel, and the saint defeats evil by the power of God, precisely aimed. Take that thought with you into your day. *School of Novgorod. Saint George and the Dragon. Icon. Russian State Museum, St. Petersburg, Russia. Courtesy of Scala/Art Resource.*

Fig. 4 *Anastasis*, early 14th-century fresco, covering the east wall, Museum of St. Savior in Chora, Istanbul. The word "Anastasis" (accent on the second syllable) means "Resurrection"; the picture represents the crucified Christ going to preach the gospel to the imprisoned spirits (1 Peter 3:18-22). The man and woman Christ has grasped by the wrists (notice that they are helpless to lift themselves) are Adam and Eve, shown as old because the human race is old. The bound figure lying face down beneath Christ's feet is not Satan: Byzantine craftsmen represented Satan as a jet-black, skinny figure with wings, a goat's tail, and upstanding hair (see Figure 5). The bound figure in this mural represents Death, hog-tied and defeated among the rubble of the broken doors of hell. Christ is shown as the death of death and hell's destruction. When you pray for a woman, you can look at Eve and pray that she will be lifted to God as Eve is being lifted in the icon; when you pray for a man, look at Adam and pray the same way. *Harrowing of Hell (Anastasis). Byzantine fresco in the apse of the chapel built by Theodore Metochites. c. 1310. Hora Church (kariye Djamie), Istanbul, Turkey. Courtesy of Werner Forman/Art Resource.*

Fig. 5 *The Archangel Michael,* first half of the 14th century, Pisa Gallery, Italy. Like the Holy Face icon, this is small, indicating that it was made for private devotion rather than for the wall of a church. The Archangel holds a balance scale of divine judgment with a roundel of the face of Christ Emmanuel, an icon within an icon. His lance has transfixed a tiny black figure who is a demon or Satan himself. The small white figure in the scale is a human soul. The Archangel is calm and in control and un-questionably on the winning side. Keep this picture in your mind today and see how it affects you. *Archangel Michael. Italo-Byzantine, 13th c. Museo Civico, Pisa, Italy. Courtesy of Alinari/Art Resource.*

Chapter 10

Special Situations

Whatever situation you are in, God has gone there before you, and he will meet you there (Psalm 139, especially verses 8-18).

Praying when you are sick

Being sick includes a wide range of ailments from a cold to advanced cancer. People who have never been very sick will say smilingly, "Oh, when you are lying in bed, never mind, you can always pray." To them I would say, "Do you remember what it was like the last time you had flu? You lay there feeling weak and shivery and you ached all over and everything looked far away and it hurt even to move your eyes. How much praying did you do then?" The honest answer is, "Well, not a lot."

Western medicine has lately realized that people are psychophysical units: when one part is sick, the whole person is affected. Flu is a physical illness caused by a virus. When you have it, it is difficult to think and to pray, and everything can get out of proportion. Just as physical sickness can affect the spirit, the influence can flow the other way. Deep and long-lasting guilt, whether it is justified or false, is an illness of the spirit, and someone in its grip may show physical symptoms such as insomnia or muscle stiffness. Anger that is unexpressed and unresolved can also cause physical symptoms such as stiffness or headaches, and the physical pain in such cases is as real as it would be if the pain had a physical reason.

Where Western medicine has erred for the last three hundred years is in ignoring the reality of a spiritual element in some illnesses — that is, supernatural rather than psychological. *Sometimes* people feel that they are being oppressed by demons because they *are* being oppressed by demons.

Spiritual influences that ought to be good may sometimes have a bad effect. If people are put into stress by coming under the influence of dramatic preaching, emotional religious events, or one-to-one evangelism that is unsuited to them, they may develop physical symptoms. When the soul is stressed, the body says, "Please leave me alone for a while so I can regain my sense of identity." If someone is having problems with prayer, the solution may not be still more prayer or Bible reading or the latest Christian book, but a trip to the bowling alley or the skating rink.

Intense religiosity is an illness of the spirit: the cure is having a good time with good friends. Jesus Christ was accused of being a glutton and a winebibber. Because it was his critics who said it, we can take their words with a grain of salt, while the truth at the heart of their words is that he knew how to enjoy himself.

Praying when you have been bereaved

In bereavement the mind of a Christian is like the mind of anyone else: it shuts off. If you can find someone to confide in, you may say, "I don't know why, but I can't even pray." That is normal. The conscious levels of the mind have been anaesthetized by shock while God is at work deeper inside, helping the bereaved person to come to terms with the terrible blow. Healing will begin from the deep levels if you take time to be quiet and let it happen. For the time being, prayer must be allowed to be very simple and probably will be without words. You can always touch the hem of Jesus' robe, and if even that simple act of faith seems too hard, a long look at him will be enough. If even looking takes too much out of you, curl up near him like a tired child: he understands if that is all you can do.

Bereavement is spiritual wounding and affects you like a physical amputation or any other major surgery: you will experience physical weakness, an inability to think clearly, and mood swings between dullness and hyperactivity. Western society in the late 20th century cannot cope with death, so we are encouraged to behave as though it hasn't happened. People are congratulated for "standing up to it well," and in their grief and bewilderment they try to live up to their friends' expectations, thinking that this is what they ought to do.

By contrast, orthodox Jews let themselves grieve for a solid week, sitting still and quiet. They sit on a low chair, bringing their body into the fetal position — which is exactly how an emotionally shattered person wants to sit. They maintain silence, eat simple food, wash only basically, and simply exist while the hours pass.

They don't first organize the things in the desk, the will, the personal possessions, the lawyers, the clothes, the books, or the emotional relatives who seem to have moved in permanently.

Bereaved Jews who follow their tradition seriously do not *first* do *anything*. The day after the funeral they sit still and quiet for seven days, just staring at the walls. It is a form of spiritual hibernation and is exactly what you would do if you had received a deep physical wound. After the week, they set aside a further thirty days for a less intense period of grieving before they begin to emerge again into daily life.

It is like emerging into consciousness after surgery: first the dazed hours when you slip into and out of consciousness, then the longer recuperative time when you feel yourself very slowly growing stronger. If you were visiting a friend in the hospital after major surgery, you wouldn't say, "Snap out of it!" or "You must make all these new, difficult decisions *first* and *then* go on a lively holiday!" or "Let it all out: have one good cry, then get on with your life!" or "Don't just sit around. Do something to take you out of yourself!" (What a violent phrase that is.)

Someone who has received a physical wound needs time to rest, to be still and quiet, taking time to come to terms with it. They need that recuperative time immediately after the wound, and so it is with someone who has suffered the spiritual wound of bereavement. Even if you were bereaved years ago and the wound is still painful, consider taking a week to sit in silence. Your priest or minister may be able to recommend a place for you to retreat to. The natural reaction to bereavement is to sit still for a while and just stare at the walls, so give yourself the opportunity to do it. It is not "moping": it is allowing healing to begin to happen.

Praying when you are in physical pain

Physical pain is tiring, and this is when the prayer of smiles and glances comes into its own, because the prayer is very simple and takes only minimal effort. It is all you can do, which means it is like the widow's mite: the greatest that you can do. When you are in physical pain, the prayers of other people will become more important than ever, because they hold you up when you haven't the strength to hold yourself. Give yourself into the hands of praying friends just as you give your body into the hands of the doctor and nurses who care for you. The commitment is like an exhaled breath, slight and deliberate: "I trust other people's prayers; I am in their care now." You may find that you need to repeat this act of commitment, gently and repeatedly, until it becomes a direction of the mind. It is like being a secure and happy child again, being settled into bed and tucked up by other people's prayers. This is the experience of intercession: you are now on the receiving end.

Praying when something difficult happens

God does not owe any of us a perfectly happy life, smooth, prosperous, unruffled, and glistening with grace. We are not big fat swans gliding on a lake, but pilgrims stumbling along a road that may be very rough indeed. Sometimes the only positive thing that can come out of a difficult time is that you went on believing that God meant it for good.

"How long, O Lord? Not long, because no lie can live forever. How long, O Lord? Not long, because mine eyes have seen the glory of the coming of the Lord" (Martin Luther King).

Praying with someone who is dying

I held a friend's hand while she was dying and taught her the Jesus Prayer, timing it to the rhythm of her quick, painful breathing; in her case it took four breaths in and out to each repetition of the set of words. I told her, "To breathe is to pray." She was barely conscious and was unable to speak or to do more than move her eyes and the fingers of one hand, but I know she heard and I know she understood and I know she was helped. "Lord Jesus Christ . . . Son of the Father . . . have mercy . . . upon us. . . . Lord Jesus Christ . . . Son of the Father . . . have mercy . . . upon us. . . ."

One of her friends, a member of the Dutch Reformed church, came and stood by the bed, staring and very quiet. "I never heard anyone praying like that. It's — *beautiful.*"

Praying when you are never alone

As someone who is renewed by solitude, I find the continual presence of other people extremely debilitating. To be with people every hour, day and night, feels as though I am being sucked dry, leaving only a husk. That could be because I am an only child, or maybe simply because of my personality. Some people are renewed by being with others, and for them it is solitude that is disturbing and threatening.

Whatever kind of person God made you to be, the kind of praying I have been writing about is the solitary kind. So how do you pray on those days when you are never alone? That is the time for the prayer of smiles and glances and for the Jesus Prayer, brief, heartfelt, and direct; it is possible to slip it into an under-level of consciousness and to continue to pray like that when you are chatting to someone. God hears your prayer, and that is what matters.

Praying when you have been mugged or robbed

You are precious in his sight. That is the thought to hold onto for however many hours, days, weeks, months, or years it takes to come to terms with the experience of being mugged or robbed. You are precious in his sight. Don't try to dredge up feelings of love or forgiveness for your attacker or for the violater of your home and possessions, but concentrate on your own inner rehabilitation before God. You are precious in his sight. You have been wounded, whether physically or emotionally or through losing your possessions, and you need time for that wound to heal to a mere scar. Till then, prayer will be interrupted by flashbacks and lack of concentration, but you are precious in his sight.

Society beyond the Christian community has recognized the need for victim-support groups, and you should consider taking advantage of their wisdom and experience. You are precious in his sight. Healing and mental stability *will* come, however long it takes. You are precious in his sight.

Praying in very deep depression

Some modern books imply that being a Christian means always feeling good about yourself, that a proper believer should have high self-esteem, a great sense of personal direction, a happy face, a song and a prayer for every occasion. The history of God's people teaches otherwise: none of us should think ourselves exempt from the Dark Night of the Soul.

"Suddenly I saw myself on the edge of a cliff and everything was pitch black and my feet were ready to step over the edge."

"Everything was grey. I was in a grey mist. I couldn't see or feel anything front or back or right or left. It was just all grey. I couldn't move. There was no future or past. I've never been so completely without hope."

"You see, I didn't dare to start crying because I knew if I started I'd never stop. I was afraid to start."

People in that state need the healing power of silence and arms around them. If they are naturally shy, they need the healing power of silence and a hand held. If any prayer words are familiar, they need to hear them spoken slowly and gently, their mind echoing the words that they have learned many years before. They need the combination of emotional space and a friend nearby, which is achieved by having someone quiet in the house day and night, available if needed but never crashing into their wound with "Hey, let's go shopping! You need to get out of yourself!" Those in deep depression already feel that they are out of themselves, that normality has gone for good, and that only drugged unconsciousness or suicide will take the pain away. You can pray *for* someone in that state, but when all their consciousness is knotted up in raw psychic pain, they cannot pray for themselves.

Depression can enter the whole person by the body (some physical illness or physical reaction to drugs), or by the mind (after-effects of bereavement, intense worry, or fear), or by the spirit (guilt, loss of faith, or an evil influence). Whatever the point of entry, the whole person will be affected, sooner or later. What is the best way to help?

1. Physical contact: arms around, or a hand held. If there is the smallest chance that physical contact will be misunderstood, just sit nearby. Depressed persons' minds are very confused, both in actuality and in memory. They get things far out of proportion, so it is best to err on the side of extreme caution. "Give no offence in anything, that the ministry be not blamed" (2 Corinthians 6:3).

2. Take two breaths before you say anything, then again two breaths before you say anything else. This will give the person's tangled mind the time to absorb your words, and it will bring your conversation down to the person's speed rather than yours. It will also give you time to think about what you are going to say.

3. Instead of trying to analyze how the depression entered this personality, minister to all parts as well as you are able.

4. Never say, "I know how you feel," or even, "I can imagine how you feel," *unless you have had an identical experience.* The person in deep darkness knows very well that you don't know, and the claim that you do, or that you can imagine it, throws up a barrier between you. Be honest. Say something like, "I can't begin even to imagine how you feel. I only know you need to be helped, and I am here for you."

Praying when you have failed

Mother Teresa has said, "The Lord did not call me to be successful: he called me to be faithful." Many Christians are faithful in ways that only God knows about, working on and on without recognition or public acclaim. Others try to work but fail all too publicly.

To acknowledge personal failure is difficult, more so in some cultures than in others. Watch children in a well-equipped playground, active little people of different ages and abilities climbing, swinging, and jumping. One child wants to do something on a piece of climbing equipment and launches himself at it with joy. Yes, of course he can, everything in him tells him that he can. Seconds later he is face down on the dusty ground, sobbing. He failed and the whole world saw it. What does a wise parent do? A wise parent picks him up, wipes his face, and says, "Now try something else that you *can* do, and do it well."

So you failed. You wanted to do something and it didn't work out as planned, but now you can succeed in forgiving yourself for having failed, even if it is a difficult task that may take days, weeks, months, or years. God is a wise parent who wipes all tears from our eyes.

Chapter 11

When Praying Is Boring or Difficult

You are simple flesh and blood, so don't expect to be able to pray equally well every day. Some Christians think of themselves like a double-decker London bus: what they call their "real life" is on one level, while what they call their "spiritual life" is somewhere up on another level. When they can't feel the presence of God, they begin to worry about whether there is some hidden sin. Their reasoning runs like this: "Prayer is a spiritual activity; so if it is difficult, there must be a spiritual reason." In fact the reason may be a lack of sleep, but that doesn't sound so interesting.

When God sometimes seems absent, don't worry: you have felt something that is part of ordinary Christian experience. It is not constant, but it is normal in the sense that every praying person goes through it again and again, sometimes for long periods. Sometimes God seems absent because he *is* absent — not in the sense of having lost interest in you but because he is training you to walk by yourself. Watch a daddy helping a child to ride her first two-wheel bike. To begin with, he holds the handle-bars steady while the child peddles and wobbles, then he withdraws his hands and the child rides alone. He knows best when he can take his hands away.

God's help is as strong as mountains, and you will find it is there when you need it, but not whenever you whine for it. For now, devote your energies to going on as steadily as you can without becoming disheartened. Try repeating a form of words over and over again, very slowly, or simply concentrate on being as near to God as you can without striving for conversation in either direction.

St. Francis de Sales wrote:

> . . . think how many courtiers go into the presence of the prince hundreds of times without any hope of speaking to him but only to be seen by him and to pay their respects. In the same way, Philothea, we come to prayer, purely and simply to pay our respects to God and to prove our loyalty. (*Introduction to the Devout Life*)

Prayer can be boring or difficult for the most or-dinary reasons. Here are sixteen reasons listed more or less from the simple to the complex.

Stiffness

Maybe your body wants to move. If it is not allowed to, the mind moves instead and concentration flies out of the window. The solution is to let the body move, change your position or stand up to stretch, or take yourself for a walk, praying as you go.

If your everyday job involves a lot of sitting, your muscles will cry out for more to do. You may have given up a weekly game of golf or tennis because the pressure of work made it seem wrong to take the time, but work can be wrong if there is too much of it. God instituted the Sabbath, and we need to structure little Sabbaths into everyday life. You may not impress people with what a busy Christian you are, but you will accomplish more of quality in God's service.

Physical tiredness

Are you getting enough sleep? We must be good stewards of our flesh and blood. Recognize how much sleep you need and take practical steps to be sure you get it. The part of us that St. Francis of Assisi called "Brother Donkey" needs to be stabled, rubbed down, and fed; he also needs time to graze in a pleasant pasture, time to enjoy life, and time to play. Look after Brother Donkey: he is part of the whole person who prays.

Proper diet

Are you eating properly? Indigestion or anemia or a drastic change of diet will upset your whole body and will therefore affect your ability to pray. It is not only the soul that prays, it is the whole of you.

Room temperature

Your concentration will be ragged if the room you are praying in is uncomfortable. Is it too hot so that you feel drowsy, or too cold so that you feel fidgety? If you find it is difficult to pray, the temperature in the room may be the simple reason with an equally simple solution.

Interruptions

This is one of the most common problems. You may go into a church to pray, but interruptions occur as people practice the organ or hold meetings or run vacuum cleaners; find out when these things normally happen so you can avoid them. At home you may have an answering machine, but you can't eliminate the doorbell. Your place for praying won't be perfect, because this isn't a perfect world. So stop thinking, "If only I had a monastic cell to retreat to — *then* I could pray properly."

When the doorbell rings, take a deep breath before going to answer it. Move without tension or hurry, return to prayer immediately after the interruption has been dealt with, and expect to spend some time gathering up your quietness again.

Overwork

To be well used in God's service sometimes means to be tired. But think carefully about whether you may in fact be overreaching yourself. Neither animal, human, nor machine can do more than its proper share of work, and we vary in our capacity. Christians are good at making their fellow believers feel guilty about not taking on more work. "Oh, there is such a *need* . . ." they will say, and people who are already working to their full capacity — or beyond it — will sigh and take on even more. The fact is that God has other workers besides you, and if a job is within his plan, someone will step forward to do it. Relax: you couldn't save the world if you worked twenty-four hours a day for the rest of your earthly life. Do what you can and offer it to God at the end of each day.

If you are depressed in comparing yourself with some other Christian, I hope you soon learn that such comparisons are a waste of time. Some people are able to work all day, all night, and most of the next day. Others simply can't. Taking on more and more responsibilities is a fine boost to the ego, but you can only do what you can do. If people demand more, let that be their problem, not yours.

Change

It is normal to go through a slump after a major change in your life. We expect it after sudden sorrow like bereavement or loss of a job, but it is also normal after a happy change that has been planned for some time, such as marriage or a new job. Instead of trying to keep up the pace, retreat a little, settling for a shorter time to pray and using the simplest forms you know; in time you will be able to get back to where you were. When your mind has received a jolt, it will slip back to the most familiar forms. When I began writing this chapter, I heard of the death of a much loved aunt-in-law. All the prayer I could manage that day was a few minutes of wordless sorrow with the Lord's Prayer, a Collect, and intercession for two people who were on my mind.

A balanced life

Are you trying to pray too much? It is possible to become prayer-centered in the wrong way. A better balance in your activities may be all you need for your prayers to take wings.

Fear

In sudden fear prayer goes back to the earliest, simplest forms we knew. People who memorized prayers in childhood are to be envied, because they always have something to go home to; even though it may not be word-perfect, scraps and shards will remain. I remember saying the Lord's Prayer and the Creed over and over again when I was lost in a swamp in Cornwall one dark evening. Familiar words kept me going for the two hours that it took before my feet felt solid ground again.

Some people speak to God only when they face a major crisis, and they then go back to the simple religious words that they learned twenty or even fifty years before. That may be because prayer is an unfamiliar exercise, but certainly it is also because everyone's mind in crisis behaves like that of a frightened child. When fear comes, let the child in you speak to God in little broken phrases and silences and bits of childhood hymns. It is prayer. It will be heard.

The occult

If you have ever touched the occult and have not vowed to avoid it completely, it will be one reason why you can't pray as well as you wish. It doesn't matter if your contact with darkness was socially acceptable, or described as "just a bit of fun" like going to a fairground fortune-teller. Vow to remove it from your life from this day on: no ifs, ands, or buts, get rid of every shred. That includes never again reading the horoscopes in the daily paper. If you can still say to yourself, "Oh, this doesn't count, this is harmless," you are still facing in the wrong direction and the Devil is smiling at you. People who turn to the occult want to get in touch with the supernatural in a materialistic society. Christians know how to get in touch with the supernatural in God's way, and relate themselves to that winning side.

Late-medieval and early Renaissance cartographers sometimes wrote words of warning near the edges of their maps, "Here be dragons." Those maps placed Jerusalem, God's city, in the center of the world, and we retain a memory of that when we speak of the East or the West, meaning east or west of Jerusalem. Medieval mariners understood that dragons and demons belonged on the outer edges of things and were best left alone.

Doubt

People turn doubt into defensiveness because no one prepared them for it and they are afraid, thinking there is something abnormal about them. They behave like a child who hides himself in a closet and shouts to all who come near, "I'm all right! Nothing is wrong! I don't need help!"

Our society idolizes honesty in religion, suggesting that people with doubts are hypocrites if they pray or go to church, but that is the Devil's reasoning. If you have doubts, it is best to put yourself into the place where those doubts can be resolved into faith. Church attendance and private prayer are two influences that will bring you — or bring you back — to belief. To stay away would be like refusing to see a doctor until you felt completely well, or were nearly dead. I once had a landlady who was always complaining about her aches and pains. "Why don't you go to the doctor?" I asked her. "Oh no, dear, I'm not bad enough for that. When I can't move, then I'll go."

Doubt is one of the ways in which God teaches people. You and I have to learn to fix our faith on him rather than on an exciting preacher or a technique of apologetics or a new way of worship or the warmth of Christian fellowship. There are times when we have to go on *as though* we believed, even though we don't.

In one of C. S. Lewis's Narnia books (all of which I strongly recommend for adult reading), Puddleglum, the Prince, and the children are being drugged by the insidious rationalism of the witch who has imprisoned them underground. She asks them, teasingly, what a sun is, and they say it is like the dim lamp in the cave only much bigger. She asks what a lion is, and they tell her it is like a cat only much bigger. She tells them that her underground world is all that exists and that the great open-air world of Narnia is only their imagination. "Well, 'tis a pretty make-believe, though, to say truth, it would suit you all better if you were younger."

The children's faith in Narnia is all but gone until Puddleglum cries, "Suppose this black pit of a kingdom of yours *is* the only world. Well, it strikes me as a pretty poor one. . . . I'm on Aslan's side even if there isn't any Aslan to lead it. I'm going to live as like a Narnian as I can even if there isn't any Narnia" *(The Silver Chair)*.

That is very different from the conviction of Job, "I know that my Redeemer lives" (Job 19:25) or of St. Paul, "I know whom I have believed and am convinced that he is able to guard what I have entrusted to him for that day" (2 Timothy 1:12). But the Gospel According to Puddleglum is where our minds must sometimes live.

Imagination

We all know how thoughts can play havoc with the moments designed to be most full of grace. Your thoughts may be sensual or evil or filled with hatred; there are times when we can all feel shocked and degraded by the products of our imaginations.

When you feel joy in worship, your body wants to join in and express joy in a physical way. When your thoughts distress you, there is little to be gained by trying to suppress them or trying to concentrate on purity. Instead, give your physical part something to concentrate on. If you are kneeling, feel the floor beneath your knees and the toes of your shoes, feel every point of contact where your hands cover your face, become conscious of the table or pew under your folded hands; if you are walking, make yourself vividly aware of your clothes next to your skin and concentrate on the feel of the ground beneath your shoes. If you have a picture to look at, concentrate on it; if your church has devotional objects or movements to look at, or something to smell, concentrate on them. All these sensations are the reality and goodness of the physical world that God has made.

Gather up all your immediate experiences of touch and texture and make them an offering of joy. In spite of the Fall, this world is good and God is in it; there is no need to try to escape it when you pray. When your thoughts distress you, remember that some of the most beautiful things in the world are the products of human imagination.

The need to listen

Maybe you cannot concentrate because there is something that God wants to talk to you about but you keep changing the subject. This can result in a flurry of prayers. You wallow in a detailed monologue or you recite beautiful words with great piety and diligence, handing God flowery compliments, never letting him get a word in sideways. Take time to listen and don't be afraid.

Resentment

Prayer may be difficult because there is someone you need to forgive. This is a hard feeling to live with, especially on those occasions when you have been deeply wronged. One solution I have found is to pray for someone you dislike (Chapter 8), though the problem may not be resolved for many months. Worry is also a form of resentment; it comes from not trusting God to lead you through the life that he chooses and not trusting that he is in control when you cannot see the way ahead.

Forgiving God

You must resign yourself to walking a long, hard road if you need to forgive God. God's motive is love, even though this may sometimes be hard to see. After conversion we are still ourselves, trailing our personal histories like shadows behind us. Don't expect too much of yourself too soon or expect to be able to accept God's ways without a murmur. He doesn't change personalities; he redeems them.

Tuning and retuning

Prayer may be boring or difficult for any number of reasons; I have listed the most ordinary ones first. If several seem to apply in your case, begin by correcting the one of least spiritual interest, such as the need to get enough sleep or exercise. This is a check to make sure you are not diagnosing something glamorous to flatter your religious ego. There is no foolproof system that will make prayer easy; it is a matter of tuning and retuning each aspect until you reach a point of harmony.

Make use of what helpful tips you can; above all, aim for a steadier lasting strength rather than a dramatic boost of adrenalin. If you crack a whip over an overloaded and starving donkey, he will break into a shambling trot for a few yards and then relapse into his previous pace. No matter how elegant the whip, it will do no lasting good if what Brother Donkey really needs is rest, a good meal, time to enjoy his life, and a burden that is not too heavy to be borne.

Praying for guidance

Prayer may be difficult because a decision is weighing on you and you do not know which way to go. Personal guidance from God is something we would like often but need seldom; many Christians live their whole pilgrimage without it. For everyone to whom God spoke directly, there were many who loved and followed him by faith rather than by sight. Instead of asking for special signs, they trusted what he had already said. Would we like dramatic guidance with angels' voices and lights in the sky? Of course: it would feed our spiritual ego. But the more exact the signs we ask for, the more we lay ourselves open to events' betraying us. There are few decisions in which we do not favor one alternative over the others. If God's will is not clear, we must walk by faith as he has clearly told us to do.

The emphasis of the New Testament and of many writers since is on being established in faith, holding to sound doctrine, and living out the love of Christ in everyday life. What it all comes down to is the familiar hymn "Trust and Obey." If you already favor one of several godly alternatives, it is probably God telling you which way to go, without fuss or drama or special signs. You might not feel joy every time you make the right decision. Personal guidance sounds exciting, but there is a danger that we look at *it* more than at God.

When what we thought was guidance leads no-where, we try to forget how clear it seemed at the time. When someone admits, "I was sure it was God's will, but it turned out wrong," that is the whisper of a bruised reed. We may say that what we prayed for was God's will but that the Devil stopped it. It is more likely that we misinterpreted events. The Devil has no real victories: since the Resurrection his work has been only the scorched-earth policy of a defeated enemy.

As we spend time with God, we learn to perceive his will a little better. It is a slower process than personal leading by verses or signs, less flattering to the spiritual ego, and, most of the time, not exciting. For those rea-sons I believe it is the better path to follow. The Bible has guidelines of precept and example, and the long-established moral standards of the church set boundaries that prevent us from reaching for new definitions of right and wrong.

✛   ✛

It is the whole person who prays, a creature of flesh and blood, hopes, doubts, discouragements, fears, memories, and scars. We wait for "the glory that will be revealed in us . . . and the glorious freedom of the children of God" (Romans 8:18, 21). For now, each of us has private demons that pursue us, and we may have to live with them for a lifetime. Grace allows us to do no more than clip their wings.

Chapter 12

Praying with Other People

Mark Twain said that the "we" form of English should be spoken only by married people, an editor, or someone with tapeworm. He could have added, "and by a Christian who prays."

No Christian can pray alone, even if no other person is visible in the pew or in the room. Every Christian is part of all the rest. The great reality is that we are united in Christ whether we like it or not. Since we belong to him, we belong to one another, inevitably and eternally. One outworking of that reality is that even in our private prayers we are part of a communion of saints who pray with us and for us.

Another outworking of the reality is of course in our prayers together in groups. Praying with others can be a strengthening experience, or it can make your toes curl with embarrassment: the difference comes partly from how you were raised and partly from the way you are. The first time I was asked to pray aloud in a roomful of people I burst into tears and said I didn't know how. In subsequent months and years I forced myself to do it, because it was obviously something that was expected.

I now recognize that praying aloud in the presence of others is not my way and may never be. You must accept yourself the way you are and accept other people the way they are: there is greater love in that than in church conformity.

The verse used to justify praying in a group is Matthew 18:20. It has been quoted so many times with reference to prayer groups that it comes as a shock to people when they realize that the verse, in context, is not about prayer. It is about dealing with a brother who has offended against you. Always see a verse in context.

Taking Matthew 18:20 out of its context reinforces a common misunderstanding of prayer. God is no more ready to hear the prayers of several people in a room than of one person in a room alone. Clean hands, a pure heart, and conformity to God's will: these are what makes a prayer effective, and the Bible teaches it from one end to the other.

Conversational prayer

Sometimes a group may agree to pray about one topic at a time. Everyone feels free to contribute a sentence if they want to, but without the phrase "in Jesus' name," or "Amen" as a signal meaning, "I've finished." Each person's single sentence is *short*. There are no furthermores, or finallys, or "and we would also pray for. . . ."

People pray in any order. No one knows who will speak next any more than anyone would know in an ordinary conversation among friends. If someone has more than one sentence to contribute on a topic, that person can speak more than once, but only one short sentence at a time so others can have their turn.

Conversational prayer encourages the inexperienced and the shy, it involves everyone in the room, it keeps prayer to one topic at a time, and it encourages normal speech patterns. It restrains the wordier members of the group from going on and on and on. Have you ever been in a prayer meeting, mentally composing your own prayer (rather than listening to the others in the room) — then finding that "your" topic has already been prayed for? Conversational prayer, one topic at a time, one sentence at a time, cuts through all that.

Conversational prayer may be what some people need to help open them up after years of speaking either in set forms or in pious, loose verbiage. This method should be tried with particular sensitivity if members of the group are new to Christianity or have a tendency to fly off into emotional free-association. I suggest that the group be grounded by finally reciting together a form that they all know, such as the Grace or the Lord's Prayer.

Praying for the wrong reasons

Even if most people in the group remain silent, prayer may be happening. If those who pray aloud do so mainly to keep themselves awake, it would be better for them to go home and get the proper rest that Brother Donkey needs. Another danger of a prayer meeting is that the people are really talking to one another and that the "blessing" and "strengthening" they experience is not so much supernatural as therapeutic. There is also a danger of praying in order to impress others in the room with your faith and fervor. I have done this in the past, so I know it can happen.

Praying in tongues

The Apostle Paul laid down practical guidelines for the exercise of the gift "when you come together" (1 Corinthians 14:26 and following). We presume he was referring to public worship on the Christian Sabbath. Should his guidelines also be observed in a small prayer meeting? The answer should be either a clear yes or a clear no; talk it over in the group and be sure that everyone feels comfortable about which decision you reach — or at least are willing to abide by it rather than not coming any more if their opinion was not chosen.

Prayer gossip

A group of praying friends can be a splendid support; they can also spread gossip under the guise of sharing needs for prayer. In Matthew 18 we are told that if a brother offends against you, the first step is to speak to him directly and to him only. Not to bear false witness against your neighbor is one of the Ten Commandments: God hates gossip that much.

Even though your information about someone may be true, if there is the smallest doubt in your mind as to whether that person would like it to be known, then be silent. Here is some advice from the 2nd century B.C.:

To delight in wickedness is to court condemnation,
but evil loses its hold on the man who hates gossip.
Never repeat what you hear,
and you will never be the loser.
Tell no tales about friend or foe;
unless silence makes you an accomplice,
        never betray a man's secret.
Suppose he has heard you and learnt
        to distrust you,
he will seize the first chance to show his hatred.
Have you heard a rumour? Let it die with you.
Never fear, it will not make you burst.
A fool with a secret goes through agony
like a woman in childbirth.
As painful as an arrow through the thigh
is a rumour in the heart of a fool.

(Ecclesiasticus 19:5-12)

Notice the wisdom of "unless silence makes you an accomplice, never betray a man's secret." If you know for certain that, for example, someone molests children, you should make it known in the right quarters (and in the right quarters *only*), because if you were silent and a child were abused, God's judgment would be on you too. But as to the vast majority of pieces of information you receive, let them die with you and you will not burst.

Even without prelimary gossip, prayers themselves can become garrulously informative: "Lord, we ask you for Jim, Lord, who has lost his job because of suspected stealing, and for his girlfriend, Lord, who thinks she might be pregnant and it might not be his baby. And we would ask you, Lord, for my neighbor Mrs. Jones, who lives at the end of the road, Lord, who is into demon worship. And, Lord, we would pray for little Billy, Lord, who told me in Sunday School that his dad has a girlfriend and his mommy doesn't know, Lord."

People who pray like that are taking God's name in vain. They believe they are praying, but they are really handing out tasty bits of gossip to the others in the room. If prayers in a group are becoming more and more chatty and detailed, it is an indication that you need to enlarge them to include silence and praise, and to pray in biblical patterns as I suggested in Chapter 6.

The wonderful fact is that you need to know almost nothing about someone in order to pray for that person. When you pray for others regularly, knowing only their name and their need (told to you in perhaps only two or three words), you will find that a great love for them will grow. I cannot explain this: you will find in practice that it is true.

Chapter 13

Praying in Church

There is no perfect church, no perfect congregation, and no perfect minister or priest. For all that, we have to believe that we are members of one another and practice it, because the Bible teaches it. Every Christian needs a place to worship regularly, and a spiritual shepherd to go to when things are hard. It is not enough to drift from one church to another with the permanent attitude of, "No thanks, I'm just looking." You need to be able to name the place and to name the shepherd. Without commitment to a church, private prayer will either fade away or turn weird.

Each chapter in this book has been about an aspect of public as well as of private prayer. What is true of people on their knees in their own homes is true also of people on their knees in their pews: the same things hinder and the same things help.

Glancing prayers

When nothing much seems to be happening in a worship service, you can put your mind on God very simply with smiles and glances. You can relax a little, but without losing your thoughts to irrelevances like chatting to people on either side of you while the collection is being taken. The most fruitful time to shake hands is before the liturgy or after it when you can really meet people.

Time and place

The discipline that you practice in setting aside a time every day is the same that you need to organize your time on Sunday morning or evening. A local, rather than a distant church will be an advantage to you, because it is easy to resent attending public worship if getting there and getting home takes half the day.

Choreography and dancing

Movement in worship can become a great issue among Christians who think that it must be all-or-nothing. Members of one congregation say with pride, "*We* have dancing in the aisles in *our* church!" and members of another congregation reply with equal pride, "Well, *we don't!*" Something that might have enriched everyone's worship has become a point of division. When the angels look at us, do they laugh or cry?

When Michal saw King David dancing before the Lord, she despised him in her heart (2 Samuel 6:14-16). Today's liturgical enthusiasts have decided that she was wrong and he was right, but I wonder if we are too quick to despise Michal. Maybe David's religious enthusiasm had gone over the top. He was not incapable of doing unwise things. The natural choreography of formal worship is one thing (Ronald Knox wrote a book that recognized liturgical choreography: *The Mass in Slow Motion*), but any kind of dancing that calls attention to itself or causes embarrassment and distraction is an unwise addition to Christian worship.

Wherever there are human beings they communicate with movements and positions, and wherever they meet for worship they perform movements together even if it is no more than "Let us all rise." In that sense, every church has some form of choreography.

Informality and structure

Public worship includes informal and structured prayers. While some churches have no liturgy as such, few churches have no predictable order at all in their worship week by week. A pattern settles and unites the congregation. If most of the prayers are formal, there will be moments for informal ones in your heart.

From several years' experience in both nonliturgical and liturgical worship, I must confess that it is as easy for my mind to wander in an informal as in a formal service.

Your part in the whole

An entire service can be an act of intercession for one friend, or one problem, or one offering of praise. Sometimes a service is built around a central theme such as

Christmas; at other times you can bring your own single thought to the church and let every part of the service relate to it. A familiar liturgy is an advantage in this, since you know what words are coming next and you can let your mind swing back to its intercessory center again and again like a compass needle finding its rest at North.

Prayer without words

If there is incense, your nose has an opportunity to worship. If there are colors, ritual movement, pictures, or images, your eyes can join in as well. To sit, stand, or kneel when others do is a choreographic statement of unity with others and with the flow of the liturgy.

Many physical things can either distract you or lead you to God: the stained-glass windows, this week's flower arrangement, the architecture, the reverent beauty of an ancient liturgy, the novelty of a modern form of words. All these things are part of God's good world, and if you try to ignore their influence, it will be like trying to ignore the force of gravity. They are there to be used: the Ministry of Things should be like the preaching of John the Baptist, who pointed his followers to Christ.

Difficulties

Churchgoing can be boring or difficult for any of the reasons listed in Chapter 11; just as it is Brother Donkey who prays at home, it is Brother Donkey who trots to church.

Feeling stiff?

If you feel physically restless, get your circulation going earlier in the morning. Your muscles are crying out for use. Maybe you could walk to church or drive only partway, instead of driving door-to-door as though you had wooden legs.

Feeling tired of church?

It may be because you may be going through a slump, which is a form of spiritual weariness. It is a normal letdown and can be valuable because it makes you begin to rely on God instead of on your feelings of being religious. Welcome it and grow with it.

Are you too hot or too cold?

Simple things like being too hot or too cold in church are spiritually distracting. Dress appropriately and comfortably and be alert for sources of draughts so you can sit away from them. If you walk to church in the rain, take a pair of dry shoes to change into; it is wretched having to sit for an hour and a half with damp feet.

Churchgoing after a major change or bereavement

Whether it is physical or emotional, a major change will play havoc with your powers of concentration. Before

God, accept such upheaval as perfectly natural. Perhaps for the time being the Sunday evening services would be less taxing for you, or a midweek service with fewer people attending. If you have been bereaved and find the music in church unbearably emotional, sit at the back so you can slip out afterwards without having to meet people. Stay in touch with regular worship and ease back to full participation at your own speed.

Resentment

If you feel you cannot worship because someone in the congregation annoys you, put that name on your prayer list at once. We are real people who must learn to live and pray in a real world. Praying is practical.

Trying to pray in church when you have small children

Some of these next paragraphs may be controversial so please consider them quietly. I write as a mother who has gone through the situations I describe.

Some churches have nurseries, children's worship programs, or other alternatives for small children. In others, children are expected to sit through the service with the adults. In such churches, the chief source of interruptions for anyone in public worship is from children with their short attention span and their uncontrolled movements and voices. They are not to be blamed because they are the way they are, but because public worship is important, they should not be allowed to spoil it for others. Be honest: are you able to take part in the service if your little ones are with you, or are you continually looking around to shush them or to grab them? It would be better to defer whole-family churchgoing until the youngest member of the family is able to sit still and be quiet. Churchgoing can be presented as something special to look forward to "when you are old enough," maybe at the seventh birthday. The younger sibling would envy the one who was old enough to go with the grown-ups.

If your church does not have a Sunday School, or nursery, or if your child sincerely hates them, a solution might be to trade babysitting with a neighbor so each set of parents or single parent can attend an undistracted service once every two weeks.

Since a young child's shoes are often the noisiest part of him, take them off before he swings them against the pew. Children vary in their abilities, so do not feel discouraged by other adults telling you what *they* achieved when *their* children were the age that yours are now.

There is no automatic spiritual influence in taking the children to church once a week. Knowing that churchgoing is important to parents will make a more positive impression on a young child than being dressed up and dragged there, only to be shushed and grabbed at for an hour and a half every week.

You do not take a very young child to a symphony concert or an elegant restaurant, because it would not be fair to the child or to the other people there. So why take a young wriggler to church? You say, "To learn about Jesus." But they don't — not if they are bored and fretful and spend their time climbing over the pews and being scolded. If you want them to love good music, you play it at home as a normal part of daily life. If you want them to enjoy good food, you serve it at home rather than having just a hamburger or a TV dinner. If you want them to love Christ, teach them at home, read Bible stories, pray with them, sing choruses and simple hymns. Christianity is not for Sunday only.

To let them sit in church armed with books or paper dolls (or even with Sunday School books) and let them chatter softly while you try to attend would be using God's house as a babysitter. Even worse than that, it would be teaching them that what they can do in church is ignore the service and amuse themselves. They will not catch worship in some mysterious fashion by having it floating above their heads while they are busy dressing a doll. If they come with you, they should be expected to take part. A high church may have an advantage over a low church because there is more going on visually, and the children's attention is caught and held. Orthodox churches do not have fixed pews; most adults stand, some sit on chairs over to one side; children stand or sit on the ground or move around freely, watching the beautiful liturgy with wide eyes.

Jesus' words "Let the little children come to me, and do not hinder them" (Matthew 19:14) should be taken seriously, but they do not justify bringing little ones to any and every church service. Some churches have a service during the week that is designed for children. Take Jesus' words seriously at home. What do the children see *at home* of prayer, of a love of the Bible, of a serious consideration of how to live as a Christian in a difficult society, of consideration for neighbors, of respect and care for all people? It is *much* harder to show children these things, seven days a week, year in and year out, than just to be a nicely dressed, smiling, regular churchgoing family.

Postscript

I said at the beginning of this book that I believe regular daily prayer is practical in your life, whatever kind of life you are living now. The objections and excuses and problems about praying every day can be dealt with in down-to-earth ways. Are you still not sure? Maybe it is because the real reason for not praying has begun to emerge from the thicket of excuses: you are not quite convinced that prayer makes any difference.

You can test the strength of faith by seeing how much of it is left when it impinges on daily life. Most of the time heaven seems very far away; suppose our great gamble on faith and truth is all for nothing and we have chosen to waste our one and only life before annihilation catches up with us? Suppose that it is pie in the sky after all — in other words, nothing? Even if we are beyond that level of doubt, we all find that it is nicer to toy with some easy form of prayer from time to time than to get down to the strenuous simplicity of the real thing. Why does anyone pray? People pray because they believe it makes a difference.

You and I belong to Christ for better or worse, for

richer or poorer, in sickness or in health, to love, honor and obey, now and forever. Conversion is not the end; it is only the end of the beginning, and we are taking the first steps in the most amazing and most important relationship there is. When we pray, we come to someone who is absolutely uncontrollable and absolutely good.

I once heard a minister say something that I thought, at the time, simplistic and stupid. Now the more I think about it, the more I am coming to believe that he was right. "You never get beyond the fact that God is really there."

The Eighteen Benedictions *(Amidah)* and Prayers from the Orthodox Church and the Catholic Church

The Eighteen Benedictions

> *Some time after the destruction of the Temple in Jerusalem in 70 A.D., a 19th benediction was added after number 12. Benedictions 13 to 18 were re-numbered, but the title, Eighteen Benedictions, was not changed. I have omitted the extra prayer to give only the original eighteen.*

From the Authorised Daily Prayer Book, 1959

1. Lord, open thou my lips and my mouth shall declare thy praise.

Blessed art thou, O Lord our God and God of our fathers, God of Abraham, God of Isaac, and God of Jacob, the great, mighty, and revered God, the most high God, who bestowest lovingkindnesses, and art Master of all things; who rememberest the pious deeds of the patriarchs, and in love wilt bring a redeemer to their children's children for thy Name's sake.

2. O King, Helper, Saviour and Shield. Blessed art thou, O Lord, the Shield of Abraham.

Thou, O Lord, art mighty for ever, thou revivest the dead, thou art mighty to save.

Thou sustainest the living with lovingkindness, revivest the dead with great mercy, supportest the falling, healest the sick, freest the bound, and keepest faith to them that sleep in the dust. Who is like unto thee, Lord of mighty acts, and who resemblest thee, O King, who orderest death and restorest life, and causest salvation to spring forth?

Yea, faithful art thou to revive the dead. Blessed art thou, O Lord, who revivest the dead.

3. We will sanctify thy Name in the world even as they sanctify it in the highest heavens, as it is written by the hand of thy prophet: And they called one to the other and said, Holy, holy, holy is the Lord of hosts; the whole earth is full of his glory.

Those over against them say, Blessed. Blessed be the glory of the Lord from his place.

And in thy holy words it is written, saying, The Lord shall reign for ever, thy God, O Zion, unto all generations. Praise ye the Lord.

Unto all generations we will declare thy greatness, and to all eternity we will proclaim thy holiness, and thy praise, O our God, shall not depart from our mouth for ever, for thou are a great and holy God and King. Blessed art thou, O Lord, the holy God.

Thou art holy, and thy Name is holy, and the holy praise thee daily. Blessed art thou, O Lord, the holy God.

4. Thou favorest man with knowledge, and teachest mortals understanding. O favor us with knowledge, un-

derstanding and discernment from thee. Blessed art thou, O Lord, gracious giver of knowledge.

5. Cause us to return, O our Father, unto thy Torah; draw us near, O our King, unto thy service, and bring us back in perfect repentance unto thy presence. Blessed art thou, O Lord, who delightest in repentance.

6. Forgive us, O our Father, for we have sinned; pardon us, O our King, for we have transgressed; for thou dost pardon and forgive. Blessed art thou, O Lord, who art gracious, and dost abundantly forgive.

7. Look upon our affliction and plead our cause, and redeem us speedily for thy Name's sake; for thou art a mighty Redeemer. Blessed art thou, O Lord, the Redeemer of Israel.

8. Heal us, O Lord, and we shall be healed; save us and we shall be saved; for thou art our praise. Grant a perfect healing to all our wounds; for thou, almighty King, art a faithful and merciful Physician. Blessed art thou, O Lord, who healest the sick of thy people Israel.

9. Bless this year unto us, O Lord our God, together with every kind of the produce thereof, for our welfare; give a blessing upon the face of the earth. O satisfy us with thy goodness, and bless our year like other good years. Blessed art thou, O Lord, who blessest the years.

10. Sound the great horn for our freedom, raise the ensign to gather our exiles, and gather us from the four corners of the earth. Blessed art thou, O Lord, who gatherest the dispersed of thy people Israel.

11. Restore our judges as in former times, and our counsellors as at the beginning; remove from us sorrow

and sighing; reign thou over us, O Lord, thou alone, in lovingkindness and tender mercy, and clear us in judgment. Blessed art thou, O Lord, the King who lovest righteousness and judgment.

12. And for slanderers let there be no hope, and let all wickedness perish as in a moment; let all thine enemies be speedily cut off, and the dominion of arrogance do thou uproot and crush; cast down and humble them speedily in our days. Blessed art thou, O Lord, who breakest the enemies and humblest the arrogant.

13. And to Jerusalem, thy city, return in mercy, and dwell therein as thou hast spoken; rebuild it soon in our days as an everlasting building, and speedily set up therein the throne of David. Blessed art thou, O Lord, who rebuildest Jerusalem.

14. Speedily cause the offspring of David, thy servant, to flourish, and lift up his glory by thy divine help because we wait for thy salvation all the day. Blessed art thou, O Lord, who causest the strength of salvation to flourish.

15. Hear our voice, O Lord our God; spare us and have mercy upon us, and accept our prayer in mercy and favor; for thou art a God who hearkenest unto prayers and supplications: from thy presence, O our King, turn us not empty away; for thou hearkenest in mercy to the prayer of thy people Israel. Blessed art thou, O Lord, who hearkenest unto prayer.

16. Accept, O Lord our God, thy people Israel and their prayer; restore the services to the inner sanctuary of thy house; receive in love and favor both the offerings of Israel and their prayer, and may the worship of thy people Israel be ever acceptable unto thee.

And let our eyes behold thy return in mercy to

Zion. Blessed art thou, O Lord, who restorest thy divine presence unto Zion.

17. We give thanks unto thee, for thou art the Lord our God and the God of our fathers for ever and ever; thou art the Rock of our lives, and Shield of our salvation through every generation. We will give thanks unto thee and declare thy praise for our lives which are committed unto thy hand, and for our souls which are in thy charge, and for thy miracles, which are daily with us, and for thy wonders and thy benefits, which are wrought at all times, evening, morning and noon. O thou who art all-good, whose mercies fail not; thou, merciful Being, whose lovingkindnesses never cease, we have ever hoped in thee.

And everything that liveth shall give thanks unto thee for ever, and shall praise thy Name in truth, O God, our salvation and our help. Blessed art thou, O Lord, whose Name is All-good, and unto whom it is becoming to give thanks.

18. (Prayer for peace). Grant peace, welfare, blessing, grace, lovingkindness and mercy unto us and unto all Israel, thy people. Bless us, O our Father, even all of us together, with the light of thy countenance; for by the light of thy countenance thou hast given us, O Lord our God, the Torah of life, lovingkindness and righteousness, blessing, mercy, life and peace; and may it be good in thy sight to bless thy people Israel at all times and in every hour with thy peace.

Blessed art thou, O Lord, who blessest thy people Israel with peace.

(Final Meditation:) O my God! guard my tongue from evil and my lips from speaking guile; and to such as curse me let my soul be dumb, yea, let my soul be unto all as the dust. Open my heart to thy Torah, and let my soul pursue thy commandments. If any design evil against me, speedily make their counsel of no effect, and frustrate their designs. Do it for the sake of thy Name, do it for the sake of thy power, do it for the sake of thy holiness, do it for the sake of thy Torah. In order that thy beloved ones may be delivered, O save by thy power, and answer me. Let the words of my mouth and the meditation of my heart be acceptable before thee, O Lord, my Rock and my Redeemer. He who maketh peace in his high places, may he make peace for us and for all Israel, and say ye, Amen.

From the Orthodox Church Easter Homily of St. John Chrysostom

So enter, all of you, into the joy of your Lord. First and last, receive your reward together. Rich and poor, dance together. Those of you who have fasted, and those who have not fasted, rejoice today. The table is fully spread, let us all enjoy it. The calf is fatted, let no one go away hungry.

No one need complain of poverty, for the universal kingdom has appeared. No one need weep for their sins, for forgiveness has risen from the grave. No one need fear death, for the Saviour's death has freed us.

He has destroyed death by suffering death.

He has pillaged hell by descending into hell.

Hell was embittered when it met you, Lord, face to face below:

embittered, because it was annihilated;

embittered, because it was mocked;

embittered, because its power was destroyed;

embittered, because it was chained up.

It received a body, and encountered God. It received earth, and confronted heaven.

O death, where is your sting? O death, where is your victory?

Christ is risen, and you are thrown down.

Christ is risen, and the demons have fallen.

Christ is risen, and the angels rejoice.

Christ is risen, and life reigns in freedom.

Christ is risen, and no one is left in the grave.

For Christ has been raised from the dead, the first fruits of those who have died. To him be glory and dominion now and for ever. Amen.

A prayer of Richard Rolle, 14th century

Sweet light, joyous light, you the unmade who made me, enlighten the contours and working of my inward eye with unmade clarity. Shine into my mind so that it is wholly cleansed and so exalted by your gifts that it rushes into the full happiness of your love. Kindle it with your sweet fire so that I may sit in you, Jesus, and rest there full of joy, walking about as if ravished by heavenly sweetness and always beholding unseen things. Let me be glad in God alone.

Bible Prayers

Every prayer in the Bible outside the Psalms is listed on the following pages: prayers, ascriptions of praise, benedictions, and blessings (but not blessings that are prophecies rather than prayers). A few are descriptions of what people prayed, or directions about what to pray for, without the exact words being specified. The context is given in parentheses, followed by a brief indication of the subject or content. Prayers in the Apocrypha begin on page 172.

Old Testament

Genesis

14:19, 20	(ch. 14)	Melchizedek blesses Abram
15:2-3, 8	(14:18–15:21)	Abram prays for a son
17:17-18	(16:1–17:22)	Abraham for Ishmael
18:23-32	(18:16-33)	— for Sodom
20:4-5	(ch. 20)	Abimelech for mercy
22:11-14	(ch. 22)	Abram's faith is tested
24:12-14, 26-27	(ch. 24)	Eliezer for guidance

25:21-22	(25:19-23)	Isaac and Rebekah for children
27:27-29		Isaac gives his blessing
32:9-12	(ch. 32)	Jacob prays before meeting Esau
48:15-16, 20	(ch. 48)	Jacob for Joseph and his sons

Exodus

3:11–4:13	(3:1–4:17)	Moses questions God's call
5:22-23	(5:10–6:8)	complains
6:12, 30	(6:5–7:7)	fears his inadequacy
15:1-19, 21	(14:21–15:21)	Song of Moses, Song of Miriam
17:4	(17:1-7)	Water from the rock
17:11-12, 15-16	(17:8-16)	Moses' hands held up
18:10, 11	(18:1-20)	Jethro's praise
22:23, 27	(22:21-27)	The cry of the oppressed
32:11-13, 31-32	(ch. 32)	Moses for the people
33:12-18	(33:7-23)	— "Show me your glory"
34:8-9	(34:1-16, 29)	— "Take us as your inheritance"

Leviticus

The sacrifices and offerings were *acted prayers*.
(See Chapter Four, "Choreography.")

Numbers

11:11-15, 21-22	(11:4-30)	Moses for meat
12:13	(ch. 12)	— for Miriam's healing
14:13-19	(14:1-24)	— appeals to God's character
16:15	(16:1-18)	— after Korah's rebellion

| 16:22 | (16:19-33) | — for mercy to the people |
| 27:15-17 | (27:12-23) | — for a successor |

Deuteronomy

3:24-25	(3:18-29)	Moses asks to see the good land
9:26-29	(9:7–10:2)	— "Do not destroy your people"
26:5-10, 13-15	(ch. 26)	The people: firstfruits; tithes
32:3-4	(31:30–32:47)	To praise God's justice
33:1-16	(32:48–33:29)	Moses' final blessing of Israel

Joshua

| 7:7-9 | (7:1-15) | Joshua's despair after defeat |

Judges

5:2-31	(chs. 4–5)	Song of Deborah
6:36-39	(ch. 6)	Gideon doubts God's promise and asks for miracle-fleeces
13:8	(ch. 13)	Manoah, Samson's father
16:28	(16:23-31)	Samson's last prayer

Ruth

| 1:8, 9; 2:4, 12, 20; 4:14 | | Benedictions & blessings |

1 Samuel

1:10-11	(1:1-20)	Hannah for a son
2:1-10	(1:21–2:11)	Hannah's song of rejoicing
3:10	(ch. 3)	God calls young Samuel

2 Samuel

| 7:18-29 | (7:1-29) | God's promise by Nathan |

| 22:2-51 | (21:14–23:7) | David for deliverance (= Psalm 18) |
| 24:10, 17 | (ch. 24) | — repents after taking a census |

1 Kings

3:6-9	(3:3-15)	Solomon for a discerning heart
8:23-53	(7:51–8:53)	— dedication of the Temple
8:56-61	(8:54-66)	— blesses Israel for all nations' sake
17:20-21	(ch. 17)	Elijah for the widow's son
18:36-37	(18:19-39)	— for victory
19:4, 10-14	(19:1-18)	— in despair

2 Kings

6:17-20	(6:8-23)	Elisha for his servant to see
19:15-19	(19:9-36)	Hezekiah for deliverance (= Isaiah 37:14-20)
20:3	(20:1-7)	— for healing (= Isaiah 38:3)

1 Chronicles

4:10	(4:9-10)	Jabez for God's blessing
14:10	(14:8-17)	(= 2 Samuel 5:19)
16:8-36	(ch. 16)	— praise (= Psalm 105:1-5; 96; 106:1, 47-48)
17:16-27	(ch. 17)	— thanksgiving (= 2 Samuel 7:18-29)
21:8, 17	(ch. 21)	— repentance (= 2 Samuel 24:10, 17)
22:11-12	(22:5-19)	— blesses Solomon
29:10-20	(chs. 28–29)	— praise (compare the Doxology at Matthew 6:13 to v. 11)

2 Chronicles

1:8-10	(1:1-13)	Solomon for wisdom (= 1 Kings 3:6-9)
6:14-42	(6:12–7:3)	— for the Temple (= 1 Kings 8:23-53)
7:3, 6	(7:1-10)	"He is good; his love endures"
7:14	(7:11-22)	God's directions for penitent prayer
14:11	(14:2-13)	"the powerless against the mighty"
20:6-13	(20:1-24)	Jehoshaphat "our eyes are upon you"
33:12-13	(33:1-20)	Manasseh (words found in the Apocrypha)

Ezra

7:27-28	(7:11-28)	Thanks for Artaxerxes' commission
8:21-23	(8:15-32)	For a safe journey
9:6-15	(ch. 9)	Confession of sin (ungodly marriages)

Nehemiah

1:5-11	(1:1–2:8)	Prayer before seeing Artaxerxes
9:5-38	(chs. 9–10)	The people's praise & confession
13:14, 22, 29, 31	(ch. 13)	"Remember me for this"

Job

1:20-21	(ch. 1)	Job in bereavement and sickness
6:8-9; 7:17-21	(chs. 4–7)	Despair & anger
9:33–10:22	(chs. 8–10)	for a mediator between him & God

13:20–14:22	(chs. 11–14)	"Why do you hide?"
16:7-8; 17:3-4	(chs. 15–17)	"My advocate pleads with God" (16:19-21)
30:20-23	(chs. 25–31)	"I cry out, but you do not answer"
40:3-5	(38:1–40:5)	"I am unworthy"
42:2-6	(40:6–42:10)	"I did not understand"

Isaiah

6:8-11	(ch. 6)	"Here am I. Send me!"
12:1-6	(chs. 11–12)	Songs of praise
24:14-16	(ch. 24)	Joy after judgment
25:1-5, 9	(ch. 25)	"A shelter from the storm"
26:1-19	(ch. 26)	"You will keep in perfect peace"
37:16-20	(chs. 36–37)	Hezekiah (= 2 Kings 19:15-19)
38:3	(ch. 38)	Hezekiah (= 2 Kings 20:3)
63:7–64:12	(chs. 63–65)	A national lament

Jeremiah

1:6	(ch. 1)	"I do not know how to speak"
3:22-25	(ch. 3)	Israel: "We will come to you"
4:10	(ch. 4 & 14:13-16 & ch. 23)	Result of false prophets
10:6-7	(10:1-16)	God and idols
10:23-25	(10:17-25)	God and justice
11:20	(ch. 11)	Vindication & vengeance
12:1-4	(ch. 12)	Question about God's justice
14:7-9, 13, 19-22	(ch. 14)	"O Lord, do something"
15:15-18	(ch. 15)	"Why is my pain unending?"

16:19-20	(ch. 16)	"To you the nations will come"
17:13-18	(ch. 17)	"Save me & I will be saved"
18:19-23	(ch. 18)	Defense against false accusation
20:7-18	(chs. 19–20)	Despair
32:17-25	(ch. 32)	Obedience without understanding

Lamentations

1:9-11, 20-22	(ch. 1)	Despair: the enemy gloats
2:20-22	(ch. 2)	Horror at God's judgment
3:8, 40-66	(ch. 3)	Complaint for God to hear
5:1-22	(ch. 4)	To be remembered & restored

Ezekiel

4:14	(ch. 4)	Revulsion at God's instruction
9:8	(ch. 9)	Horror at destruction of Jerusalem
11:13	(ch. 11)	Despair over death of a friend
20:49	(20:45-49)	Dismay at lack of belief

Daniel

2:19-23	(ch. 2)	Thanksgiving for answered prayer
6:10	(ch. 6)	Giving thanks three times a day
9:4-19	(ch. 9)	Confession on behalf of the people
10:2, 12	(ch. 10)	Fasting & prayer

Hosea

| 14:2-3 | (14:1-9) | "In you the fatherless find compassion" |

Joel

| 1:19-20 | (1:15–2:32) | Prayer at a time of drought |

Amos

| 7:2, 5 | (7:1-9) | Prayer for mercy, not judgment |

Jonah

1:14	(ch. 1)	Sailors not to be held responsible
2:2-9	(chs. 1–2)	"From the depths I called"
4:2-3, 9	(chs. 3–4)	Anger at God's compassion

Micah

| 7:18-20 | (7:7-20) | "Who is a God like you?" |

Habakkuk

1:2-4	(1:1-11)	"Why make me look at injustice?"
1:12–2:1	(1:12–2:3)	"Why be silent about the wicked?"
3:2-19	(2:4–3:19)	For patience

Zechariah

| 1:12 | (ch. 1) | An angel prays for God's people |

Malachi

| 1:10-11; 2:13, 17 | (chs. 1–3) | Useless prayer wearies God |
| 3:16 | (3:16–4:5) | Conversation before the Lord |

New Testament

Matthew

| 6:9-13 | (6:5-18) | The Lord's model prayer |
| 11:25-26 | (11:20-30) | Jesus, "I praise you, Father" |

| 26:39, 42 | (26:26-56) | — in Gethsemane |
| 27:46 | (27:37-54) | — Cry of Dereliction (Psalm 22:1) |

Mark

| 14:36 | (14:22-52) | Jesus, in Gethsemane |
| 15:34 | (15:33-39) | — cry of Dereliction (Psalm 22:1) |

Luke

1:46-55	(1:26-56)	Mary, *Magnificat*
1:68-79	(1:57-80)	Zechariah
2:29-32	(2:21-40)	Simeon, *Nunc dimittis*
10:21	(10:1-23)	Jesus, "I praise you, Father"
11:2-4	(11:1-13)	The Lord's model prayer
18:11-13	(18:9-14)	The Pharisee & the Tax Collector
22:42	(22:14-53)	Jesus, in Gethsemane
23:34	(23:33-43)	— "Father, forgive them"
23:42	(23:39-43)	The thief, "Lord, remember me"
23:46	(23:39-43)	"Father, into your hands"

John

11:41-42	(11:1-44)	Jesus, outside Lazarus' tomb
12:27-28	(12:20-36)	— "Now my heart is troubled"
17:1-26	(16:28–18:3)	— The High Priestly Prayer

Acts

1:24-25	(1:21-26)	Choosing Judas' replacement
4:24-30	(4:1-31)	For boldness & power
7:59, 60	(6:8–8:1)	Stephen, while being stoned
9:5	(9:1-9)	Saul (Paul), "Who are you, Lord?"
9:10-14	(9:10-25)	Ananias
10:3, 14	(ch. 10)	Cornelius & Peter

Romans

1:7-10	(1:6-13)	"I thank . . . I remember . . . I pray"
8:15	(8:1-27)	Christians cry, "Abba, Father"
10:1	(9:30–10:4)	For Israel's salvation
15:5-6, 13	(15:1-13)	For Christian unity & peace
15:30-33	(15:17-33)	Requests for prayer
16:25-27	(16:20-27)	Final blessing & praise

1 Corinthians

1:3-4	(1:2-9)	"I always thank God for you"

2 Corinthians

1:2-4	(1:1-11)	"The God of all comfort"
12:8	(12:7-10)	Paul's thorn in the flesh
13:14	(13:11-14)	*The Grace*

Galatians

1:3-5; 6:18	(chs. 1–6)	"Grace to you"

Ephesians

1:2-3, 15-19	(1:1–2:10)	"Praise . . . thanks . . . asking"
3:1, 14-21	(2:11–3:21)	"For this reason . . . I pray" [see 2:11-22 for the reason]
5:20	(5:18-20)	"Sing & make music"
6:18-20	(6:10-20)	"Pray that words may be given me"
6:23-24	(6:21-24)	"Peace . . . love . . . grace"

Philippians

1:2-6, 9-11	(1:1-11)	"I always pray with joy"

| 4:6 | (4:4-9) | Pray with thanksgiving |
| 4:20, 23 | (4:18-23) | "To God be glory" |

Colossians

| 1:2-5, 9-12 | (1:1-14) | Praying with thankfulness |
| 4:2-4, 18 | (ch. 4) | "Pray that God may open a door" |

1 Thessalonians

1:1-3	(ch. 1)	"We thank God, mentioning you"
2:13, 3:9-13	(chs. 2–3)	"May your love increase"
5:23, 28	(5:16-28)	"May God sanctify you"

2 Thessalonians

1:2-3, 11-12	(ch. 1)	"Your faith is growing"
2:16-17	(2:13-17)	"Encourage your hearts"
3:1-2, 5	(3:1-5)	"May the Lord direct your hearts"

1 Timothy

1:2, 12	(1:1-14)	"Grace, mercy, and peace"
1:17	(1:15-17)	"Now to the King eternal"
2:1-2	(2:1-8)	"For all those in authority"
4:4-5	(4:1-6)	Receive with thanks what God created
6:15-16, 21	(6:11-21)	"To him be honor & might forever"

2 Timothy

| 1:2-3 | (ch. 1) | "I thank God . . . as I remember you" |
| 4:18, 22 | (4:16-22) | Confidence, praise, benediction |

Titus

1:4	(1:3-4)	"Grace & peace"
3:15	(3:14-15)	"with you all"

Philemon

vv. 3-6, 22, 25	(vv. 1-25)	"Be active in sharing your faith"

Hebrews

1:10-12	(ch. 1)	quoting Psalm 102:25-27
13:15, 20-21, 25	(13:11-25)	"May God equip you with everything good"

James

1:5-8	(1:2-8)	Ask God for wisdom
4:2-3	(4:1-10)	Ask with right motives
5:13-16	(5:13-19)	Pray, sing, ask for prayer

1 Peter

1:2-3	(1:1-9)	Praise for mercy
5:10-11, 14	(5:6-14)	Endurance in suffering

2 Peter

1:2	(1:1-4)	"Grace & peace in abundance"
3:18	(3:17-18)	"Grow in Christ. To him be glory"

1 John

1:9	(1:5–2:3)	Assurance in confessing sin
5:14-15	(5:13-21)	Assurance in approaching God

2 John

v. 3	(vv. 1-6)	"Grace, mercy, & peace"

3 John

vv. 2, 14	(vv. 1-4, 14)	Prayer for a friend's health

Jude

v. 2	(vv. 1-2)	"Mercy, peace, & love"
vv. 24-25	(vv. 20-25)	"To him who is able to keep you"

Revelation

1:4-6	(1:1-8)	Greetings & praise
4:8, 11	(ch. 4)	"Holy, holy, holy"
5:9-14	(ch. 5)	Praise of the Lamb
6:10	(6:9-11)	"How long, Sovereign Lord?"
7:10	(ch. 7)	Every nation, tribe, people, & language
7:12	(ch. 7)	Angels worship
11:17-18	(11:15-19)	Thanksgiving of the elders
15:3-4	(15:1-8)	"All nations will worship"
16:5-7	(ch. 16)	God's judgments are just
19:1-8	(ch. 19)	A multitude shouting Hallelujah
22:20, 21	(22:12-21)	"Amen. Come, Lord Jesus"

Some prayers in the Apocrypha

1 Esdras

8:74-90	(65-96)	Esdras confesses the people's sins

2 Esdras

3:4-36	(3:1–4:2)	"weigh our sins in the balance"

Tobit

3:2-6	(3:1-6)	Tobit prays for righteousness
3:11-15	(3:7-17)	Sarah, for her good reputation
8:5-8	(8:1-8)	Tobit (son) for life in marriage
8:15-17	(vv. 1-8)	Raguel's praise for God's compassion
13:1-18		Tobit's prayer of rejoicing

Judith

9:2-14	(vv. 1-14)	Help for the oppressed

Esther

13:9-17	(13:1-18)	Mordecai for mercy
14:3-19	(14:1-11)	For mercy from the righteous God

Wisdom

9:1-18	A ruler's prayer for Wisdom

Sirach

23:1-6	For a blameless life
36:1-17	For God's power over nations
51:1-12	Thanks for deliverance

Baruch

2:11–3:8	(1:15–3:8)	Confession and prayer for mercy

Three Holy Children

1:3-22, 29-62   Praise

Susannah

vv. 42-43   (vv. 31-49)   Against false witness

Prayer of Manasseh

"All the host of heaven
sings thy praise"

2 Maccabees

1:2-6   (1:1-10)   Jews in Jerusalem pray for
Jews in Egypt

1:24-29   (1:10-31)   "Set free the slaves"

3 Maccabees

2:2-20   (1:16–2:24)   "Let your mercy overtake us"

Index